When Hope Grows Weary
Tyronza, Arkansas and Its Place in History

Cindy Grisham

Copyright © 2013 Cindy Grisham
All rights reserved.
ISBN: 10:1492806374
ISBN-13:9781492806370

Dedication

To John and Teddy, for the stories.

Contents

Acknowledgements	4
Forward: The Place	8
Chapter 1: In the Beginning	14
Chapter 2: Founding Mother	25
Chapter 3: Little Town in the Delta	40
Chapter 4: Boom, Bust, and Trouble	58
Chapter 5: Memories and Conspiracies	76
Chapter 6: A New Generation Emerges	90
Chapter 7: World War II and the Delta	98
Chapter 8: Times of Change	111
Chapter 9: The Aftermath	121
Appendix: Searching for Mrs. Stalker	126
Bibliography	161

Acknowledgements

The journey to this completed project has been long and not without a few bumps, a couple of forks in the road, and several dead ends. The outcome, however, has been good and the trip one of much learning, laughter, and joy. Throughout the process there were many people who contributed their ideas, support, and expertise and who made the expedition worthwhile. There are a few special people that I wish to acknowledge for without them, this project would never have reached its end.

First and foremost, I wish to thank two women who guided me through the academic process from start to finish. My academic advisor at Missouri State University-West Plains, Dr. Kathleen Morrison, was the person who suggested that I should go to graduate school. Without her encouragement and prodding, none of this would have been possible. It is my desire that my work to get to this point, as well as everything that comes after it, meets with her approval. Dr. Carol A. O'Connor, Interim Dean of the College of Humanities and Social Sciences at Arkansas State University, served as my dissertation chair and saw me through to the end. Her gentle guidance, willing ear, and easy laugh, made the process less daunting. I hope the result is worthy of her many hours of time and attention.

Dr. Deborah Chappell-Traylor saw me through more Heritage Studies courses than any other professor and her knowledge, enthusiasm, and encouragement are greatly appreciated. Dr. Ruth Hawkins served not only as a committee member but as my graduate assistant supervisor at the Southern Tenant Farmers Museum. She kept me at Tyronza even when I begged to leave, and I did beg on more than one occasion. I hope this dissertation clarifies some of the issues that we all dealt with while a part of the project.

Dr. Brady Banta provided his encouragement and knowledge to the cause as well. His wonderful lectures and classroom discussions were a joy to me, and have made me a better researcher and historian. I hope the result is up to his standards. Dr. Rick Burns taught me how to do good field work and encouraged the research process along new and different lines. I greatly appreciate his assistance and support. While I never had the privilege of sitting in one of his classes, Dr. Clyde A. Milner II also deserves a note of thanks for his encouragement and support of all of the heritage studies students. Finally, I wish to thank two women whose assistance with the less exciting side of heritage studies made graduate school more bearable. Terry Thomas and Laura Surdyk provided much needed administrative support and a friendly smile when I needed it most.

The road to heritage studies took a detour through the political science department. Many thanks are due there to the wonderful people who made my transition to graduate school enjoyable and fulfilling. Dr. Charles Hartwig, Dr. Cathy Reese, Dr. Will McLean, Dr. Ross Marlay, and least but certainly not least, Dr. Richard Wang, deserve a special note of thanks for their encouragement, friendship, and grand discussions on all things political and historical. They taught me much and provided wonderful emotional support and for that I am most grateful.

The people of Tyronza, Arkansas also deserve a special note of thanks for they are the ones who allowed me to dig into their lives and the lives of those who lived there before them, in search of answers to a question they never asked to have answered. They are many and I cannot even attempt to mention everyone here, but several deserve singular notice. John Wayne Austin was the driving force behind the creation of the Southern Tenant Farmers Museum and his many hours of conversation about the lives of those who made the town their home were a joy. Teddy Prestidge was on the opposite side of the museum fight and was a hard man to get to know, but we finally achieved a friendship that I will always cherish. I look forward to many more hours of conversation with both of them. Barbara Ross and Thelma Jett both provided much assistance and guidance as I maneuvered my way through the process. They were always ready with an answer to a question or an introduction to a potential source. Thanks also go to Reeder and Shirley Smith for their knowledge and encouragement, and Marion Burke for putting up with my endless questions while he was trying to work or just sit and enjoy the afternoon. George Beley allowed me to invade his office one morning unannounced and not only made me feel welcome, but answered every question with knowledge and insight. Special thanks go to the ladies at the Midway Café who not only answered questions and entertained me with their antics, but also kept me fed with their daily special that always included pie. Linda Hinton, assistant director of the Southern Tenant Farmers Museum was always willing to work on photos and help track down sources and her husband Carroll, was a willing reader of an earlier draft and helped me get the more recent history correct. Finally, R.D. and Hilda Gill also contributed a great deal to this book. R.D. added answers and told stories and Hilda supplied the hilarity and the town is a sadder place with both of them gone.

    My friend and colleague Marjorie Hunter deserves many good wishes and thanks for her weekly trips with me from Parkin to Jonesboro during a long year of writing and research. Other friends and colleagues that deserve a thank you are Rachel Reynolds-Luster, Dr. Guy Lancaster, Jodi Morris, Dr. Lisa Perry, Leslie Hester, Faye Futch, Isaac Ongoa, Dr. Lenore Shoults, Dr. Jeff Mitchem, and Marlon Mowdy.

Finally, I have to thank my family for their love and support during my academic quest. My mother, Freda Grisham, not only had to work with me at STFM, but spend countless hours listening to me recite Tyronza findings after work. She and my late father both provided a love of all things historical and political and I will always appreciate them for that gift. I only wish he were here to see this journey come to an end. My brother Greg was always there to discuss issues and direct me to books that would improve the product. His knowledge of Southern history is second to none. I want to thank Kayla, my beautiful, red-haired girl, for putting up with my presence and many times my foul temper when I was stressed. You are an exceptional young woman and I appreciate and love you more than you know. To Tim, the love of my life and soul-mate, a special thank you for the long hours and many miles that we have traveled together. I would not have made it without you. Finally, a special thank you to my dog Jack, who kept me calm during long days of research and writing with his gentle snoring as he slept with his head on my foot, and for always knowing when it was time to take me out for a walk. I love you all.

This whole town does look like whatever hope becomes after it begins to weary a little, then weary a little more. But hope deferred is still hope. I love this town.

Marilynne Robinson
Gilead (2004)

Forward
The Place

A place that was lived in is like a fire that never goes out. It flares up, it smolders for a time, it is fanned or smothered by circumstance, but its being is intact, forever fluttering within it, the result of some original ignition. Sometimes it gives out glory, sometimes its little light must be sought out to be seen, small and tender as a candle flame, but as certain.

> Eudora Welty
> "Some Notes on River Country" (1944)

The Delta region of northeast Arkansas around Tyronza is flat; flat and level, without anything to draw the eye, save the flatness. It has been made flatter still by the monster tractors that have been prowling the land for the last couple of generations, scraping and smoothing the soil to make it easier to farm. Easier for the water to pool, or drain, or whatever it is that the cultivator of that particular plot of land wants it to do. It is this flatness that creates a sense of the place that is void of any identity worth remembering. A land so vast and plain that even most of those who call it home cannot appreciate it for anything other than as a factory to produce their crops or to collect their subsidy checks.

This part of the Delta does not have the Deep South feel that permeates the air in the more southern reaches of the place. A drive through southeast Arkansas, on the lower side of Interstate 40, what my friend Norwood calls "South of 40", can transport the traveler to another time on a warm summer evening. The hot, sticky air combined with the sight of old sharecropper shacks and plantation commissaries falling into decay makes you feel like you are in an old Robert Johnson song. Large old homes belonging to the planter class still dot the small towns that linger along the vast stretches of two-lane highway that crisscross South of 40. You can easily see the past in these little towns because you have to slow down. Slow down for the boys playing basketball in the street, for the elderly woman carrying her groceries home from the store, for the old dog sauntering down to the courthouse to get his back scratched by one of the loafers, for they are still there. The south has a reputation for being slow and somewhat lazy, but I can tell you from experience that slow is the only way to survive it.

The heat and humidity during the long, hot Arkansas Delta summers on both sides of Interstate 40, even when the rain is not falling, take their toll on people. The air is so think with moisture that it seems more sensible to try to drink it rather than breathe it. This kind of climate, while not hospitable to people is very friendly to flying things such as mosquitoes, biting flies, and other insects. A novice to the region while trying to drink in some of the moist air has to take care not to take in a winged creature or two. During their first drive down a Delta highway in the evening they usually think they have encountered a sunlit hailstorm before they realize that the thuds hitting the car are bugs. Southern humorist Julia Reed in her book *Queen of the Turtle Derby and Other Southern Phenomenon* said that it is the heat, humidity, mud, bugs, and crawling creatures that make living in the Delta akin to living in the Old Testament. Both are full of plagues and pestilence.[1]

---

[1] Reed also believes that the high rates of alcohol consumption in the Delta can also be blamed on mud, rising water, snakes, malaria, and heat. She believes that liquor is the only thing that makes it tolerable. The title of her book interestingly enough, comes from the annual Terrapin Derby held every year now since 1936 in the east Poinsett County town of Lepanto, just a few miles up the road from Tyronza.

But the northeast quadrant of Arkansas, where Tyronza lies, is squarely in the Delta without the depth of Euro-American history that accompanies the regions settled before the Civil War. In the overall history of the Delta this land is new and fresh. The fortunes made here were those made by upstarts from the mountain south or the Midwest who moved in carpetbagger-like after the railroads opened it up and built towns and lives from the mud and the swamps. It is new money and the sordid stories that always accompany a fortune being made. It is here, in this "new" land, that this story takes place.

When you first arrive in eastern Poinsett County, it is difficult to picture this place as it was when first the Ohio River and then the Mississippi, cut their channels through this land leaving the smaller rivers like the St. Francis, the Little, and the Tyronza to fill their old beds. Hard to imagine how it appeared to the aboriginal peoples who moved in and built their mounds and planted their fields and created a civilization in the bend of a river that no longer bends, but that has been cut-off and channelized so that it runs straight instead of following the natural curves and turns that the rivers in this valley have followed naturally for millennia. It is difficult to imagine the stands of cypress and oak and tulip poplar and other hardwoods that stood tall in the swampy terrain that was left behind after the big earthquakes of two hundred years ago. A place where old steam engines pulled their loads of timber on temporary tracks that crisscrossed the land. It is all so flat now.

There is a small rounded mound near the exit off of U.S. Highway 63 that leads into downtown Tyronza. It sits in a large field, usually planted in cotton, and has a handful of trees and four white granite stones that mark the graves of some of the town's early settlers. While it is no more than twelve feet higher than the land it sits on, it commands attention. It is high ground and the most visible evidence that someone once occupied this land before the here and now. It survived because it held the bodies of white settlers, the East family who arrived in the 1890s and whose descendants would leave less visible, but just as important, marks on the town. This mound is now the property of an East descendant again. Great grandson George Beley purchased the land where the mound sits back a few years ago from the Norcross family, who had obtained it years ago from his grandmother who had gambled on a crop of cotton one year and lost. She lost the land and the family graves and it was George Beley's goal to get that land back, and he did.

The mound was a constructed place as well although it seems as much a part of the landscape as if it had always been there, but it was not. Built by a group of people we now call Mississippians for their civilization situated up and down the length of the Mississippi River Valley, this mound was a part of a vast community that occupied the bend in the Tyronza River where it joined Dead Timber Lake. The river was straightened just above this bend at a place now called the Tyronza Cut-Off to alleviate the flooding that the modern town dealt with early on in its existence. Dead Timber Lake is only a small remnant of its former self, mostly dry and a victim first of drainage then of leveling. At one time though, before the region was settled and the timber cut, the rivers straightened, and the land drained; it was a tremendous body of water.

Officially, U.S. Highway 63 cuts right through the city limits of Tyronza into the heart of the town. In reality the roadbed leaves the town in its wake. Bypassed and appearing deserted, it sits unnoticed by most travelers who drive the route. They have heard of Tyronza but have never taken the time to drive into it. They feel they have no reason to. The town sits near to the ground on a visible horizon that is already low, with a line of one story buildings, and some trees in front of the railroad track that is really the only elevated thing, but it is flat and level as well and is not noticeable either. The only things that truly stand out are the twin water towers each standing slightly above the town on their four steel legs, one old and one new, both simply bearing the name TYRONZA.

Although it is hard to believe when you look at the town today, it was once a busy, bustling place. Uncle Billy Beasley was one of those who came into the region as a young man, looking for work and adventure. I do not know about adventure, but he found work at least with one of the first of the Poinsett County timber men, Oliver Davis, and before he was finished had married the boss's daughter, a girl named Ella. He ended up learning the business, buying up more land, and building an empire of lumber. He and Ella lived in a lovely Victorian home on Beasley Street near the school and church. His Tyronza Lumber and Cooperage Company operated a lumber mill and a slack-cooperage in Tyronza for twenty years and he often traveled around the country attending to his business and going to conventions. By 1910 he had logged all of his holdings and was in the process of selling the land to the hundreds of men, women (for in Arkansas a woman could own her own land), and families who flooded the Delta looking for land to grow that most magical of all crops, cotton.

The house is gone now and Beasley Street functions as little more than an alley behind the last remaining Main Street businesses, the sole remaining physical manifestation of Uncle Billy. I read in an interview with Clay East that the Davis and Beasley mill's sawdust pile covered almost fifteen acres of land and that it caught fire one day and smoldered for five years. On a warm winter's day not long ago, Teddy Prestidge told me the same story. Uncle Billy and his empire still live on in Teddy's mind. You can see it in his eyes when he looks around. In some small way, even though I never witnessed it with my own eyes, I can still see it as well.

Judy Perry Black grew up in nearby Marked Tree, but was the granddaughter of Tyronza banker, planter, and merchant John A. Emrich. She and her brother Ed, the children of Emrich's daughter Sarah and her husband Ed Perry, Sr., recalled stories of Tyronza and their family for me in a visit at her home in Cherry Valley. The two spent almost every day in Tyronza interacting with their mother's siblings and their families. Judy recalled that three of the Emrich sisters, their mother Sara, as well as Margaret and Dorothy, would meet every afternoon at the Little Red Inn for coffee to listen to the farmers talk and discuss the family business. The family business was not so much the financial side of life but the emotional side. She described the town as "exciting" with all of the farmers gathering in the heat of the day to discuss crops and equipment, and the townspeople going about their business, not in Jonesboro or Memphis, but in Tyronza. Saturdays exhibited a carnival type atmosphere with the sharecroppers and tenants coming in from out in the country to spend the day; shopping, eating out, visiting with friends, and going to movies.[2] George Beley related similar stories of living in the town. He and lifelong resident John Wayne Austin both tell the story of a shooting by the city marshal of a local planter's son over sixty years after it occurred with such detail that it might have happened only yesterday. They all talked about the movies that were shown on the side of the Odd Fellows Hall on Saturday night, a story that was told by so many others who grew up there.

Sociologist Eugene Walter says that a place can "move the soul" without being "attractive to the senses." We are trained generally to suppress the feelings of place by looking at the logic of space; in other words, we place great emphasis on design and aesthetics. Tyronza is not much to look at, but

---

[2] Interview with Judy Perry Black, Cherry Valley, Arkansas, January 11, 2012.

there is something there. It can move the soul if you give it half a chance.

Chapter One
In the Beginning

On ground so flat and low and marshy, lies a breeding-place of fever, ague, and death. ...a dismal swamp...teeming with rank, unwholesome vegetation. ...a jungle deep and dark, with neither earth nor water at its roots, but putrid matter, formed of the pulpy offal of the two, and of their corruption.

         Charles Dickens
         Dickens on America
         (1842)

  Tyronza is called a Delta town. It sits in the southeast corner of Poinsett County, in the northeast corner of Arkansas, at the southern tip of the St. Francis Sunken Lands, which is all a part of the Mississippi Alluvial Plain, and not really a delta at all. The Mississippi Alluvial Plain begins at Thebes, Illinois, at a point just above the confluence of the Ohio and the Mississippi, and extends south to the Arkansas River. It lies in a 200-mile-wide structural depression known as the Mississippi Embayment, and covers an area of over ten million acres, and includes one-third of Arkansas's seventy-five counties.[3]

  The plain is bisected by a geologic anomaly known as Crowley's Ridge. The Ridge, as it is known locally, is a loess-topped, Tertiary monadnock, running along a north-south line paralleling the Mississippi River, and dividing the plain into two distinct halves. Between the ridge and the Ozark Highlands is an area known as the Western Lowlands. It is

---

[3] Willard B. Gatewood, "The Arkansas Delta: Deepest of the Deep South," in *Arkansas Delta: Land of Paradox,* eds. Jeannie M. Whayne and Willard B. Gatewood (Fayetteville: University of Arkansas Press, 1993), 3.

drained by the White River. The Western Lowlands include the section known as the Grand Prairie, the largest producer of rice in the United States. East of the ridge and extending to the Mississippi River lies a series of low lying areas known collectively as the Eastern Lowlands.[4] They begin at the confluence of the Ohio and Mississippi Rivers near Cairo in southern Illinois, and extend south to the mouth of the Arkansas. These lowlands are drained by the St. Francis River which enters the Mississippi River near Helena.[5] Geologists think that at one time Crowley's Ridge divided North America's two great rivers, with the Mississippi flowing through the Western Lowlands and the Ohio flowing through the Eastern Lowlands.[6]

The rivers of the plain meander along in a southerly direction, often changing course and leaving traces as they go. Flowing in an s-shaped pattern through deep, soft, easily eroded soil, the waters shape not only the physical landscape but the culture as well. The land, although appearing flat and level, consists of a series of basins, prairies, lowlands, ridges, oxbow lakes, bayous, and swamps. The rich land with its temperate climate and abundant water supply today encourages bountiful harvests of cotton, rice, soybeans, corn, and other row crops, but just over a century ago fostered majestic forests and lush native vegetation.[7]

While the richness of the land encouraged settlement and supported a thriving economic system, it was hard on the

---

[4] Michael J. O'Brien and Robert C. Dunnell, eds., *Changing Perspective on the Archaeology of the Central Mississippi River Valley*, (Tuscaloosa: University of Alabama Press, 1998), 4.
[5] Charles Hudson, *Knights of Spain, Warriors of the Sun: Hernando de Soto and the South's Ancient Chiefdoms*, (Athens: University of Georgia Press, 1997), 277.
[6] The fluvial origin of Crowley's Ridge has lately come under scrutiny as there exists evidence of recent uplift at various places along the length of the formation. The favored cause of this uplift is seismic activity along the New Madrid fault line which runs parallel to the landform.
[7] Gatewood, "The Arkansas Delta," 4.

people. Abundant rainfall each spring over the low-lying land resulted in annual flooding and overflows which threatened their lives physically. The flood waters, the only source of drinking water back then, mixed with the detritus of human habitation and resulted in a toxic brew that brought epidemics of cholera and dysentery. Unknown to the residents at the time, the stagnant pools left behind in the shallow depressions for months after the overflows, harbored mosquitoes resulting in rampant malaria. The few roads that existed when not under water were either waist deep in mud or so dry, hard, and dusty that they choked the people and animals who attempted to traverse them. A visitor to the Delta region during the Civil War reported that the region was a "vile" place where "even the snakes have chills."[8]

Tyronza sits atop a low-lying sandy ridge, which rises gently ten to fifteen feet higher than the surrounding land. This ridge covers an extensive gravel bed that is approximately one mile wide and three to four miles long, and lies inside what once was a loop of the Tyronza River.[9] Technically the loop is not the Tyronza but a combination of the Tyronza and Dead Timber Lake. Dead Timber Lake is what geologists call a terminal distributary. A distributary is a stream that steals water away from another channel. Distributaries can sometimes steal so much water away from the main river that it will become the main channel.[10] This did not occur in Dead Timber Lake because it is a terminal body meaning that it had

---

[8] Ibid, 6.
[9] Cyrus Thomas, *Report on the Mound Explorations of the Bureau of Ethnology*, (Washington, D.C.: Smithsonian Institution Press, 1985), 203.
[10] The most famous case of an American distributary is the Atchafalaya River in Louisiana along the Mississippi River system. The Atchafalaya currently receives thirty percent of the flow of the Mississippi but is restricted from taking more by the United States Army Corps of Engineers by use of both the Old River Control Structure and the Morganza Spillway. Many hydrologists believe that the Atchafalaya will eventually capture the Mississippi completely which would divert river traffic away from the busy ports of Baton Rouge and New Orleans, both of which lay downstream.

a terminus or ending point, resulting in an oxbow type lake bed. Where the lake leaves the Tyronza River, called the node, it occupies an abandoned meander loop of the Mississippi River but at some point it left the channel and spread out over the land, possibly as a result of the ground disturbance from the New Madrid earthquakes. A little over a hundred years ago though, it existed as a body of water six to eight feet deep running from its junction with the Tyronza all the way to Deckerville, four miles to the south. The work done to drain land in the early part of the twentieth century ended up lowering the levels in the Tyronza River to such an extent that Dead Timber starting flowing back into the river instead of the other way around.

Although it is difficult to visualize today on the altered landscape, the place was a naturally defensible town site. Pre-Columbian settlers in the region could see the value perhaps as far back as 1000 A.D. and established a village in the same location that the current town now occupies. This early village was the home of a mound-building society of Native American agriculturalists known as the Mississippians.

The Mississippians

The earliest people in the Central Mississippi Valley were hunters and gatherers, but localized attempts to domesticate plants began in the eastern woodlands perhaps as long ago as 2000 B.C. For generations the peoples of North America hunted animals such as the white tailed deer, rabbits, and raccoon. The people fished the rivers and naturally occurring lakes and gathered wild fruits, seeds, and nuts from the river bottoms. The women experimented with growing varieties of wild plants near their homes and successfully began raising several varieties of squash, pigweed, knotweed, marsh elder, sunflowers, and beans.[11] As these crops became a dependable

---

[11] Bruce D. Smith, "Agricultural Chiefdoms of the Eastern Woodlands" in *The Cambridge History of the Native Peoples of the Americas, Volume 1:*

source of food, permanent villages began to grow around the cultivated fields. These early settlements were small and dispersed and archaeological data shows little evidence of warfare.[12] While the region provided food for its inhabitants, they were forced to travel to obtain other items that were needed by the villagers, such as stone for tools and weapons, or desired, such as marine shell and copper for jewelry. An extensive trade system developed among the communities all along the Mississippi Valley. It was through trade with the peoples of southwestern North America that the Mississippians obtained corn (maize), a crop that would significantly alter their lives.

Because maize could be stored over a long period of time, and could be used when needed, it became a useful commodity for trade. Though long thought to be the dominant agricultural crop grown by the native peoples of North America, it did not start to attain prominence until at least 800 A.D. Stored in large pits dug into the ground, maize was a source of power for the people who could grow it successfully and the physical landscape changed into an intensive farming operation. Around 1000 A.D., the people who lived in what would one day become northeast Arkansas began to obtain a type of stone known as chert from communities in the American Bottoms in west central Illinois near present-day St. Louis. This chert was fashioned into primitive hoes which allowed the women to cultivate larger parcels of land.[13] These improved implements, combined with the introduction of maize as a food crop, brought about extensive changes in the Mississippian lifestyle.

Mississippian communities grew larger and more organized. The rise of the chiefdom directly correlates with the increase in

---

North America, eds. Bruce G. Trigger and Wilcomb E. Washbirn (New York: Cambridge University Press, 1996), 273.
[12] Hudson, *Knights of Spain,* 278.
[13] Bruce Smith, "Agricultural Chiefdoms," 276.

maize production from about 800 to 1000 A.D.[14] The early village at Tyronza appears to have been intact during the rise of maize production as evidenced by the discovery of mud casts of "gourd seed corn"[15] in the excavations of the remaining mounds by the Smithsonian's Bureau of Ethnology Mound Survey team in 1884.[16] Archaeological evidence suggests that a "long and painful transformation" occurred along the upper reaches of both the Tyronza and St. Francis Rivers and in the Cairo Lowlands of southeastern Missouri beginning about 700 to 1000 A.D. Various cultures consolidated and communities became more elaborate. Larger towns developed at strategic locations, such as Casqui at present-day Parkin in neighboring Cross County, and Pacaha near Turrell in Crittenden County.[17] Smaller villages surrounded the larger towns and small farms were scattered between the towns and villages to assist with the food supplies. The village at Tyronza was probably in this category, although the large number of mounds at the site seems to indicate that it was a large community.

The chert rock originally used for hoes and other farm implements was developed into spear and arrow points. Initially used for hunting, these points began being used for warfare between competing chiefdoms. The increase in wars brought about social stress and political turmoil. This period of unrest was accompanied by the global climate change of the

---

[14] Hudson, *Knights of Spain,* 280; and Bruce Smith, "Agricultural Chiefdoms,"268.
[15] So called because of the flat white kernals resemblance to the seeds of gourds or squash. It is available again commercially, after being thought extinct.
[16] Thomas, *Report on the Mound Explorations,"* 205.
[17] The Parkin Site is believed to be the paramount village of the chiefdom of Casqui, which is named for its chief. The site at Turrell is believed to be the paramount village of the neighboring chiefdom of Pacaha, which is also named for its chief. Both are less than twenty air miles from Tyronza.

Little Ice Age.[18] Mississippian society thrived by utilizing a system of maize production called double-cropping which meant that the long, warm growing season allowed for two complete crop cycles: a fresh or green corn season in which the ears were roasted over the fire while in the soft, milk stage; and a dry season in which the crop was allowed to complete its growth cycle until it dried on the ear. At this point it could be stored over a period of years to be used when needed. The Little Ice Age that began in about the 13th century resulted in colder, wetter, and considerably shorter growing seasons and in many cases loss of the second dry corn crop which was used to survive the winter months. Over the next four hundred years there was considerable variation in the weather patterns which resulted in reduced resources and increased competition. Many of the villages were burned, some perhaps intentionally, and by 1350 A.D. the entire Cairo Lowland, once the center of the Mississippian culture, was abandoned and had become a wilderness. The Mississippians appeared to have moved farther downstream.[19]

On June 28, 1541, the Spanish conquistador, Hernando de Soto, crossed the Mississippi River into present-day Arkansas. His crossing was believed to have taken place a little south of Memphis. De Soto's chroniclers describe the land they saw as the richest and most agriculturally productive they had observed so far in their trek across what is now the southeastern United States with impressive urban centers surrounded by agricultural fields. Towns were laid out along a series of roadways. Populations in the towns numbered in the thousands in some instances and they were filled with square-shaped, thatch-roofed houses and contained earthen mounds which housed the chief and in some cases temples.

---

[18] For a detailed look at the Little Ice Age see, Brian Fagan, *The Little Ice Age: How Climate Made History, 1300-1850.* (New York: Basic Books, 2000).
[19] Hudson, *Knights of Spain*, 280.

The Indians offered gifts of food and clothing, but the Spanish insisted on taking more by force and quickly wore out their welcome. De Soto and his men stayed in Arkansas for two years and their time there brought destruction to the native peoples. While many native people were wiped out by exposure to European diseases for which they had no immunity, these contagions most likely did not reach the Mississippi Valley. Instead Spanish warfare and demand for food in a land that had been decimated for several years by drought, probably greatly contributed to the end.[20]

By the time the next wave of explorers, the French led by Father Marquette and Louis Joliette, came through the Mississippi River Valley in 1673, the Mississippians were gone. Their villages had been abandoned, left for nature to reclaim. The agricultural fields, cultivated so carefully by Mississippian women, were left to grow up in sprouts which, helped along by the richness of the deep alluvial soil quickly became thick lush forests. The late colonial historian, Francis Jennings, said it best when he stated that Europeans did not find a virgin wilderness in America, but a widowed one instead. [21]

Whether the Tyronza site survived until the arrival of Hernando de Soto is unknown and will most likely never be determined as so little of it remains. The site lies between two prominent chiefdoms of the late Mississippian period, Casqui and Pacaha, both of which were visited by the Spanish and reported in great detail by the chroniclers of the expedition. Archeologists from the Smithsonian's Bureau of Ethnology visited the area in the early 1880s and documented its existence collecting numerous pieces that are now housed in

---

[20] De Soto's chroniclers reported that the village at Casqui (present-day Parkin) has experienced drought conditions for seven straight years.
[21] Francis Jennings, *The Invasion of America: Indians, Colonialism, and the Cant of Conquest.* (Chapel Hill: University of North Carolina Press, 2010), 15.

the Smithsonian's Museum of Natural History. Included among the pieces are items with ceramic designs that clearly indicate a late Mississippian presence, such as Parkin Punctated pottery. Ethnologists Edward Palmer and Philetus W. Norris reported that at least forty-nine mounds once dotted the land that is now Tyronza. Thirty-two of them were already gone by 1884, leveled for fill dirt by the men who constructed the rail bed for the Kansas City, Fort Scott, and Gulf Railroad.[22] The early townspeople took out the rest. Today the only visual evidence of the village site is a large mounded area, much diminished in size, with a house sitting on its top. The structure is the third such residence to occupy the site, each successive act of construction taking away more of the dirt so that today only a remnant remains.[23]

While the land that would eventually become northeastern Arkansas was rich and full of potential, the thick forests and swamps prevented much in the way of habitation from de Soto's time and for the next four hundred years. Cherokee hunting parties regularly traversed the region, setting up temporary hunting and fishing camps, but permanent settlement was short-lived at best. This was especially true in the region now known as the St. Francis Sunk Lands[24] that lie today in eastern Poinsett and Craighead Counties, and

---

[22] Cyrus Thomas. *Report on the Mound Exploratiions of the Bureau of Ethnology.* Washington, DC: Smithsonian Institution Press, 1985.

[23] Archaeologist Robert H. Lafferty, III looked at the remains of a sweat lodge from the East site, on the south side of Tyronza, which was opened as a result of the expansion of US Highway 63 and the construction of ramps at the Exit 8 interchange. Carbon dating of objects from that site show a range between 1260 and 1410 AD. The East site is not considered part of the Tyronza Mounds site visited by the Smithsonian so the date range may be different. See, Robert H. Lafferty, III, "A Mississippian Sweat Lodge," in *Architectural Variability in the Southeast,* Cameron H. Sullivan Lacquement and Robert Lynne Scott, eds., (Tuscaloosa: University of Alabama Press, 2007), 158.

[24] Modern residents are now likely to utilize the name Sunken Lands when referring to this region, but historic usage was always Sunk Lands.

western Mississippi County in northeast Arkansas. These Sunk Lands were formed primarily over thousands of years by the aggradations of the rivers in the region, but it was an event of cataclysmic proportions that contributed extensively to this unusual land formation.

Earthquake

In the early morning hours of December 16, 1811, former President of the United States Thomas Jefferson was awakened at his Virginia home, Monticello, by a sudden and violent jolt. In the capital city of Washington, D.C., the sitting president, James Madison, would also be awakened by a similar phenomenon.[25] The source of the shaking was approximately eight hundred miles to the west of the two presidents, centered in a sparsely populated part of the country acquired less than ten years earlier as a part of Jefferson's massive Louisiana Purchase.

There, in what was then the Territory of Louisiana and now southeast Missouri, residents of the little pioneer town of New Madrid reported being roused from their sleep by a tremendous crash like thunder, the beginnings of a massive earthquake. Survivors reported first a sound like a cannon or thunder followed by flashes of what appeared to be lightning that filled the sky, a sulfurous fog permeated the air, and the ground seemed to turn to liquid and roll like the ocean. Assuredly, many of those who experienced it thought the gates of Hell had opened upon them. An eyewitness account by New Madrid resident Godfrey LeSieur tells a chilling tale.

> *could neither stand nor walk. The earth was observed to roll The first shock came at 2 a.m., December 16, 1811, and was so severe that big houses and chimneys were shaken down, and at half-hour intervals light shocks were felt until 7 a.m. when a rumbling like distant thunder was*

---

[25] Alan Pell Crawford, *Twilight at Monticello: The Final Years of Thomas Jefferson.* (New York: Random House, 2008), 78.

> heard, and in about an instant the earth began to totter and shake so that persons in waves a few feet high with visible depressions between. By and by, these swells burst throwing up large volumes of water, sand, and coal.[26]

By the end of that day, twenty-seven additional aftershocks had been counted. Fifteen minutes after the eleventh quake had subsided, the river settlement of Little Prairie, located at present-day Caruthersville, Missouri, literally sank into waist deep water that reached out "as far as the eye could see." In a scene reminiscent of Moses leading his people out of the wilderness, the residents of Little Prairie, led by an elderly man named George Rodell, walked hand in hand through the water carrying their children and what few personal belongings they had managed to save for a distance of eight miles until they reached high and dry ground. They were accompanied in their trek by frightened domesticated and wild animals of all kinds, struggling along together through the cold water to reach safety.[27]

The Mississippi River also would react to the earthquakes in strange and violent ways. William Leigh Pierce, who was on a flatboat south of New Madrid when the first earthquake occurred reported in a letter to the *New York Evening News* that on that day his boat traveled fifty-two miles between seven in the morning and four o'clock that afternoon or at a speed of approximately six knots per hour. At flood stage the river runs between four and five knots per hour.[28] Over the next three months, an additional two hundred earthquakes would be counted along this stretch of the Mississippi River. At least three of them, including the initial shock, scientists now

---

[26] Edward M. Shepard, "The New Madrid Earthquake," *The Journal of Geology* 13, no. 1 (Jan-Feb 1905): 47.
[27] Jake Page and Charles Officer, *The Big One: The Earthquake that Rocked Early America and Helped Create a Science*. (Boston: Houghton Mifflin Company, 2004), 5.
[28] Margaret Ross, "The New Madrid Earthquake," *The Arkansas Historical Quarterly*, 27:2, Summer 1968, 96.

estimate were 7.0 or greater on the Richter scale, with one possibly as strong as 8.4.[29]

Throughout the Mississippi Alluvial Plain, as the ground shook the land alternately rose and fell, pushing some of the terrain up and draining bodies of water as it went, while at the same time dropping some places as much as fifty feet and creating lakes in an area where only hours earlier thick forests had existed. The shaking eventually subsided but the devastation of the country was extensive. Thick cypress swamps, shallow and crystal clear lakes, and a tangled, upended, wilderness of hardwoods stood between Crowley's Ridge and the Mississippi River after the shaking ended.

Even with the earthquakes the United States' desire to populate the lands west of the Mississippi was strong. The federal government issued bounty land certificates in exchange for military service during the War of 1812, and many of the veterans moved west to these new lands only to find them basically uninhabitable. Overflow conditions throughout the better part of the year made travel difficult, and damage to the land from the earthquakes, such as sand blows and fissures, rendered settlement almost impossible. The government was forced to trade these bounty land certificates for tracts in other locations. The area remained virtually vacant, inhabited primarily by fishermen, trappers and fur traders until the passage of the Swamp Lands Act of 1850. Under this act the federal government gave sixty-four million acres of wetlands to the states in the hope that they would encourage the organization of local drainage districts to render the land usable. Fifteen states shared in the prize

---

[29] Ibid, 98. The number of aftershocks counted in the New Madrid area was estimated to be approximately 200, but Jared Brooks of Louisville, Kentucky recorded 1,874 quakes between December 22, 1811 and March 15, 1812. It is believed that Brooks may have recorded multiple shocks that the people closer to the epicenter felt as one continuous quake. Although no large quakes were reported after February 7, 1812, residents reported small aftershocks every few days until at least 1816.

including Arkansas, receiving the third largest share of almost eight million acres. Over two hundred thousand acres of Poinsett County were included in this arrangement.[30] While some states like neighboring Missouri turned the land over to the counties for reclamation, Arkansas sold the land primarily to speculators who realized that it would someday bring a premium price.[31] One of these speculators was a man named Napoleon B. Martis. Martis had worked as a surveyor for the federal government and understood the value of the timber and fertile soil that lay over the region. He purchased thousands of acres of this northeast Arkansas swamp land after the Civil War. It was one of these tracts of land that would later become Tyronza.[32]

---

[30] Jeannie M. Whayne, *A New Plantation South: Land, Labor, and Federal Favor in Twentieth-Century Arkansas.* (Charlottesville: University of Virginia Press, 1996), 15.
[31] Hugh C. Prince, *Wetlands of the American Midwest: A Historical Geography of Changing Attitudes.* (Chicago: University of Chicago Press, 1997), 147.
[32] Abstact, Tyronza Ginning Company Papers, University of Arkansas Special Collections Division, Fayetteville, AR.

Chapter Two
Founding Mother

It had all the earmarks of a genuine, pre-1890 outpost of progress: isolation, privation, violence, ignorance, sickness and vice; few comforts, little money, and nowhere to spend it; cattle but no fences, wagons and no roads; few laws and even fewer people to administer them; plenty of outlaws, preachers, and patent-medicine peddlers, but not many doctors, teachers, or philosophers; a sparse population that was self-reliant, independent, and tough as a tempered wagon wheel.

Roy Swank
The Trail to Marked Tree
(1968)

Moving into the wilderness is not an activity for the weak of body or spirit, be they male or female. While southern women have long been stereotyped as frail and delicate flowers that spend their days doing fancywork, serving tea, and supervising those who tend the formal gardens around the mansion, in the Delta, as in many other regions of the southern United States, this image was far from accurate. Delta women spent much of their lives in extreme isolation living in dreadful conditions. They lived with mud, water, poisonous snakes, insects, disease, and disaster on a daily basis. Historian John Solomon Otto, in his definitive work on early Delta timber and logging operations, reported that the swampy land promoted mosquitoes which brought on malaria, and most settlers suffered from the disease on an annual basis. Quinine was a known cure but it was expensive and not readily available, so most people utilized home remedies with less success.[33] Delta women experienced childbirth, sickness, and death either on their own or with the assistance of whatever friend or neighbor they could find.[34] Many of them died young, leaving babies and young children. If they survived, though, they were likely to outlive many of their immediate family members including spouses and children. It is one of these survivors who figures strongly in the beginnings of the place that would become Tyronza.

She was born Martha Ann Lewis on February 23, 1836, probably in what is now Crittenden County, Arkansas, and was always known by her middle name Ann.[35] She was a pioneer from the beginning, her birth preceding statehood by almost four months. The place where her family lived, Blackfish Lake on the Crittenden and St. Francis county line, was an oxbow lake left over from one of the many times that the Mississippi changed it course. It is drained by Blackfish Bayou which eventually empties into the St. Francis River. Just ten years earlier the area had been described by a young Army engineer, Lt. Charles Thomas, as a "complete wilderness, entirely uninhabited."[36] While Crittenden County held a great deal of fertile farm land along the Mississippi and it was quickly filled with large landowners, slaveholders who grew

---

[33] John Solomon Otto, *The Final Frontiers, 1880-1930: Settling the Southern Bottom Lands.* (Westport, CT: Greenwood Press, 1999), 6. Malaria was often referred to as ague or marsh fever and its symptoms included fever, shivering, joint pain, vomiting, anemia, jaundice, retinal damage, and convulsions. The symptoms last generally from four to six hours and reappear every two to three days depending on the strain. Although a patient may eventually report the absence of the disease, one in every five patients will see symptoms reoccur the following year. In one documented case, the patient suffered every year for thirty years.
[34] Willard B. Gatewood, "The Arkansas Delta: Deepest of the Deep South," in *Arkansas Delta: Land of Paradox,* eds. Jeannie M. Whayne and Willard B. Gatewood (Fayetteville: University of Arkansas Press, 1993), 6.
[35] Scott Williams, e-mail message to author, June 7, 2010.
[36] Julia Ward Longnecker, "A Road Divided: From Memphis to Little Rock through the Great Mississippi Swamp," *The Arkansas Historical Quarterly* 44 (Autumn 1985): 208.

cotton, the Lewis family lived a row back from the big river on small acreage that the family maintained themselves. This rich, deep alluvial soil lay in a place the government maps had labeled "The Great Mississippi Swamp."

According to family lore, the Lewis family lived along the Memphis to Little Rock Military Road, the first federal highway in the state. This Military Road was a far cry from what we now think of as a highway. It was a twenty-four foot wide thoroughfare hacked through the wilderness by the Army Corps of Engineers. It took several years to build because just as soon as one section was completed water would rise over another section and destroy it. To cross Crittenden County alone required construction of three wood-framed bridges over deep bodies of water, twelve log causeways over bayous ranging anywhere from forty to sixty feet in width and not over four feet in depth, and over twenty sections of ditching alongside the road bed on the dry land.[37] Blackfish Lake and nearby Shell Lake were large enough to need ferries for crossing. Until 1860 every manner of individual traveled this road, from government officials to soldiers on their way to fight Santa Anna in Mexico. The Creek, Choctaw, Chickasaw, and Cherokee all used the road as they were marched from their homelands east of the Mississippi to the newly established Indian Lands in the west. Although she would have been very young, Ann assuredly would have watched transfixed as over six hundred fifty members of the Bell Detachment of Cherokee in their colorful turbans and clothing, the last of the seventeen groups to traverse the Trail of Tears, crossed the ferry at Blackfish Lake in late November 1838.[38]

---

[37] Longnecker, "A Road Divided," 208.
[38] Although the Creeks, Choctaws, and Chickasaws also crossed from their former homes in the southeast to Indian Territory along this stretch of road, Ann would only have been old enough to remember the Cherokee.

Ann's parents' names are unknown. Both apparently died by 1860, as their remaining children are scattered among friends and neighbors. Early census records list the names of heads of households only, with the remaining family members indicated by numbers and divided by age and gender. There are several Lewis men who could have been Ann's father based on the ages and gender of the children. Early county records are sparse or non-existent, so her childhood will probably always remain a mystery. What is known about her early life is that she married for the first time on March 4, 1857 at the Crittenden county seat of Marion to a young man named J.L. Baker.[39] In late 1858 Ann gave birth to her first child, a boy named James who was always known as Jimmy. When Jimmy was just a baby, J.L. would die of some unknown disease or accident and Ann would be left a widow at the age of 23. A year and a half later she would marry for a second time to another young neighbor, David Anthony Pittman.[40] David was a member of an established family from Mississippi who had relocated near Batesville, in Independence County. In the 1860 census he is farming rented land on Blackfish Lake with his new bride, her little boy Jimmy, and Ann's older sister Caroline.[41] Any happiness the little family had was soon to be shattered by the coming of the

---

[39] Certificate of Marriage, J.L. Baker to Martha Ann Lewis, March 4, 1857, Crittenden County, Arkansas, County Clerk's Office, Marion, Arkansas. I have found no one who can verify the given name of J.L. Baker, but he is most likely John Baker, age 19 from Illinois, who is found living with a couple named Thorn on the 1850 census for Jackson Township, Crittenden County. He is listed as a laborer. There is living nearby with a widow named Landrum, a group of Lewis children whose initials, sex, and ages roughly parallel those of Ann and her siblings.

[40] Certificate of Marriage, David A. Pittman to Martha Ann Baker, June 6, 1860, Crittenden County, Arkansas, County Clerk's Office, Marion, Arkansas.

[41] 1860 Federal Census, Jackson Township, Crittenden County, Arkansas, p. 829, family 287, Dwelling 287, lines 15-18.

Civil War, an event that divided not only the country, but families, neighbors, and communities.

When Arkansas left the federal union in May 1861, it was not without discord. Two secession conventions were held before the state decided to cast its lot with the Confederacy, and still many residents remained loyal to the Union. Among the loyalists was the Pittman family. In a letter dated September 8, 1861, David writes to his father, Ephraim, in Independence County about the flow of men out of the state to join the Confederate Army in Memphis. "I think there was 1,000 solgiers [sic] passed on to Memphis yesterday from this State there was some olde grey headed men along."[42] Hostilities escalated in the state and those loyal to the Union banded together for protection. With the arrival of the Union Army in Batesville after the Battle of Pea Ridge in Benton County, many of these men, David's father Ephraim and brother William included among their numbers, enlisted in the Union Army in the 1st Battalion Six Months Arkansas Union Infantry. The unit was marched to Helena and then placed on a steamboat for the trip to Benton Barracks, near St. Louis for training. These men never saw action, but their casualties from disease were staggering with losses nearing forty percent. Although David's name is not listed on the muster rolls for the unit, or any unit for that matter, he apparently was with the Union army in some capacity for he died in St. Louis on February 28, 1863, a full two months after the enlistments of the First Arkansas had expired. Several members of the First Arkansas perished in the weeks and months following their termination of service with the army, still in military hospitals. It is very likely that David was among them.

Ephraim and William apparently stayed with him until he died, then traveled back down the Mississippi River for home. They stopped over at Blackfish Lake to check on Ann and

---

[42] Roger Haley Howard, *The Descendants of David Anthony Pittman: Seven Generations* (Little Rock: self-published, 1984), 3.

probably to report David's death to her. Ephraim, in a letter to his wife Nancy back in Independence County dated July 18, 1863 states:

> I am at Blackfish and William is with me. William is in bad health. David is dead. He died with the measles. His family is well. Ann has a child. Its name is Nancy Caroline. Me and William will be home shortly. Try and do the best you can til I come.[43]

Ann's baby was Nancy Caroline Pittman, born nine months prior to her father's death. He possibly never knew of her birth. At the age of twenty-five, Ann was a widow for a second time, left to care for two children under the age of five in the middle of a war.

While no battles are reported to have raged within the confines of Crittenden County, life there was not easy. Partisan bands, claiming allegiance to one side or another, traveled the roads leaving terror and misery behind and the Union Army was in occupation from about 1863 through the end of the war. Ann would in her later years recount stories to her grandchildren of those she called invaders who would force their way into homes, ripping up beds and pillows searching for items of value. They would take all of the food and livestock they could eat at the time and destroy what remained to prevent the other side from getting it. She learned to hide items she treasured by wrapping them in a cotton sack and putting it down inside a "dug well."[44]

While Ann and her two children, Jimmy and Caroline, survived the war, her in-laws would not be so lucky. Ephraim Pittman implored his wife to do the best she could until he

---

[43] Howard, *The Descendants of David Anthony Pittman*, 4. The original letter at the time of the completion of the book in 1984, was in the possession of Pittman descendant, LaQuinta June Braden Montgomery of Andrews, Texas.

[44] Ibid, 6.

could come home, but he never arrived. Both father and son were captured by someone, the army, partisans, or just plain outlaws, and killed. While the location of their deaths remains a family mystery, there is some speculation that they may have occurred at Blackfish Lake. After the war, Nancy Pittman and some of her younger children traveled to the gravesites and exhumed the bodies taking them back to Independence County for burial. It seems reasonable that someone who knew and cared about the two men would have kept watch over the graves throughout the war and led the Pittman's to the site. A letter to Mrs. Pittman from one of Ann's neighbors, John Stanley states, "I have not heard from Ann in a good while. They was all sick the last time I heard from them."[45] Ann never learned to write, schools being few and far between in the wilderness. Perhaps she asked her neighbor and friend to write the letter to Mrs. Pittman informing her of her husband and son's deaths and he became the contact person for the two women.

Even after the war's end, life in Crittenden County would be far from peaceful. With former Confederates unable to vote, the electorate was sixty-seven percent African American and racial issues moved to the forefront. The Ku Klux Klan was extremely active in the county, and as a result, Arkansas's Reconstruction Governor Powell Clayton declared martial law in Crittenden and nine other counties that he deemed in a state of insurrection. Possibly among those early Klan members was the man that became Ann's third husband.

Duncan Stalker was a Canadian who had settled in Crittenden County prior to 1860 where he found work as a sawyer at one of the many sawmills operating in the county.

---

[45] Ibid, 8. The 1860 Federal Census shows a Perla Lewis, age 16, living in the Stanley household. She is thought to be Ann's younger sister, Paralee Lewis. A later letter to Mrs. Pittman from John Stanley discusses the deaths of her husband and son at the hands of a Confederate partisan band. This also supports the theory that the men were killed while at Ann's home.

He was married in June of 1860 to a woman named Elizabeth Pearson. She was a widow with three small daughters. In March of 1862, Duncan enlisted in the Confederate service in a unit known as the Crittenden Rangers, a part of the 3rd Arkansas Cavalry. He served for the duration of the war in the famed Army of Tennessee seeing action at Franklin, Chattanooga, Chickamauga, and in both the Atlanta and Carolinas Campaigns. He served for a time under the legendary cavalry officer and later founder of the Ku Klux Klan, Nathan Bedford Forrest. His own company's major was Josiah Francis Earle, who later became a notorious Klan leader in eastern Arkansas and the founder of the timber town of Earle in western Crittenden County. It was an interesting marriage for a woman who had lost her last husband to the Union cause but times were difficult and people did the best they could. A woman by herself, especially one like Ann whose parents were already dead, was often forced to enter into another marriage rather quickly and this may have been the case with Duncan.

The date of their marriage is unknown but is believed to have occurred sometime between 1867 and 1870, as their oldest surviving child was born in 1870. Daughter Caroline remembered in her later years living in a tent on the Indian mound with her mother and brother as a very young child in order to secure a homestead claim. Ann first stayed near her older sister Caroline and her family who lived north of Earle in the Gibson's Bayou community. When her sister Caroline died she and the children moved a few miles north to Poinsett County to be near her younger sister, Paralee. A federal land patent filed by Ann in 1888 contains two statements from neighbors verifying that she had been a resident of Poinsett County since 1867.[46] In April of 1876, Duncan and Ann

---

[46] Benjamin F. Webber, Testimony of Witness to fulfill the Homestead Application for The Heirs of James Baker, 25 August, 1888, General Land Office, Bureau of Land Management, National Archives, Washington, DC.,

purchased 160 acres of land from Napoleon B. Martis in southeastern Poinsett County where the town of Tyronza now stands.[47] Martis was a federal surveyor and land speculator who lived on the ridge south of Harrisburg. The day before the Stalkers purchased the land from him, he had paid back taxes on the land to the United States of America, securing ownership of the property that Ann had perhaps lived on for over ten years.

When Ann and her children first arrived in Poinsett County the area was completely forested and bore no resemblance to the wide open expanses of farm land that exists there today. Sister Paralee and her husband Jasper Mullins lived about a mile south of her on land that is now part of the Norcross farm in the vicinity of Cherry Beam Church. Also in the vicinity were the John and Rhoda Carroll family, and the Benjamin Franklin Webber family. Jasper Mullins had served alongside Duncan in the Confederate Army and could have been the reason for Duncan's arrival after the war.

In June of 1880, the federal census taker found Ann and her family living on their parcel of land in Poinsett County. It had taken the census taker three days to travel from the last home he visited to reach the family.[48] Ann was listed as a widow. The family now included a three-year-old daughter Ella, as well as ten-year-old Florence, eighteen-year-old Caroline, and twenty-one-year-old Jimmy. Also in the household was a boarder, a man named John B. Rushing whose occupation was listed as farm laborer and who was probably helping Jimmy work the farm. According to the family Bible records kept by Ann and Duncan's youngest daughter, Mary Ella Stalker Thorp, Duncan Stalker died on September 20, 1876, at the family

---

and John Christian Wilson, Testimony of Witness to fulfill the Homestead Application for The Heirs of James Baker, 25 August, 1888, General Land Office, Bureau of Land Management, National Archives, Washington, DC.
[47] Poinsett County Land Records, Deed Book B, #476.
[48] 1880 Federal Census, Little River Township, Poinsett County, Arkansas, p. 23, family 163, dwelling 163, lines 1-6.

home, just five months after he and Ann secured purchase of the land. He would have been forty years old. Ann was eight months pregnant at the time with Ella. No cause of death is listed but it could have been anything from a farming or timber accident to a fever or snakebite.[49]

America was spreading quickly to the far west during this time and the need for timber to build cities and railroads was strong. The vast Sunk Lands stand of virgin hardwood timber was coveted by Eastern interests with an eye toward profit. The stands there were considered the most important in the state with over six thousand square miles of timber.[50] The problem was getting the trees out of the swampy land and to the mills where they could be turned into houses, stores, furniture, and the hundreds of other goods that this fast-growing society craved. Timber men first tried cutting the trees from boats, then floating the logs out of the swamps,[51] to the rivers, then on to one of the many sawmills that had cropped up in the landscape. Floating worked in the spring when the rains were coming down regularly, but by midsummer, the overflow areas were a sticky, muddy quagmire and by August everything turned to a choking dust. Tram roads, also known as "dummy lines", were developed and worked like the railroads except with wooden rails that were laid on timbers. An iron-wheeled cart with flange wheels

---

[49] A few yards from the mound that Ann's home sat atop was a mound that contained the graves of "whites", according to Edward Palmer. Ann requested that the Smithsonian researchers not dig on that mound, although part of it had been destroyed by the railroad construction. I believe that since no family member has reported Duncan or Jimmy buried at Dead Timber beside Ann, that they were both buried here. The mound with its graves are now lost, a victim of agricultural practices and the construction of the Ozark Trail Highway, later designated U.S. Highway 63.
[50] Carl H. Moneyhon, *Arkansas and the New South, 1874-1929* (Fayetteville: University of Arkansas Press, 1997), 98.
[51] Clay East, interview by Sue Thrasher, September 22, 1973, interview E-0003, transcript, Southern Oral History Collection, University of North Carolina, Chapel Hill, NC.

and pulled by oxen was loaded with the logs and brought out of the woods to the mills.[52] The process worked well on a local level, but in order for the system to be efficient, the logs and finished lumber needed to be brought to the national market. The answer, of course, lay in the railroads that by this time crisscrossed the land and would soon bring new people and towns to the Sunk Lands.

From 1877 to 1900 the South built railroads faster than the national average. By 1890, nine out of ten Southerners lived in a railroad county.[53] In 1881, representatives of the Kansas City, Fort Scott, and Gulf Railroad arrived on Ann Stalker's doorstep. The route they had chosen through the swamps to the valuable river port at Memphis would travel diagonally across her 160-acre farm, cutting it in half from northwest to southeast. Almost directly in the center of the farm and very near Ann's house, stood easy access to the sand and gravel deposits that lay under the soil. Because of the problems with flooding and the annual overflows in the spring, the track would need to be built up to a height above the flood levels, and the gravel at the Stalker farm, along with the soil taken from the surrounding mounds, would greatly aid in the construction. At Duncan's death the farm had passed in part to Ann, but also to his only descendants, the two little girls Florence and Ella. An 1881 warranty deed records that a male trustee was appointed to see to the interests of the two children in conveying title of the needed land to the railroad. Ann was eventually paid one dollar for the right of way across her farm.[54]

By 1882 the railroad began opening up the Sunk Lands. In addition to the line through the Delta, the St. Louis, Iron Mountain, and Southern made its way down the ridge and the

---

[52] Ibid.
[53] Edward L. Ayers, *Southern Crossing: A History of the American South, 1877-1906* (New York: *Oxford university Press, 1998),* 7.
[54] Poinsett County Land Records.

St. Louis and Southwestern Railroad laid tracks across the prairie on the western side of Poinsett County.[55] Construction in the Tyronza area occurred during 1883 and 1884. A local woman, Anna Ritter, remembered that it was all done manually using shovels and wheelbarrows, and was a source of employment for many men.[56] Railroad construction was very dangerous work with many men crushed – resulting in lost limbs or even death, but it paid well and was eagerly sought after.[57] A depot was planned as early as 1883 approximately 100 yards down the tracks from Ann Stalker's house. Ann was now operating her home as a boarding house, providing food and shelter to the men who worked to build the rail bed. Imagining her life during this time period is difficult as little scholarship has been completed in the region on women, but an autobiography by an Arkansas woman named Mary Hamilton, written in the 1930s and published in 1992 sheds some light on Ann's daily life.

Mary operated a boardinghouse, first for the railroad then for her husband's timber camp, in neighboring Craighead County in the little town of Sedgwick from 1884 until about 1890. She worked alongside the same Kansas City, Fort Scott and Memphis Railroad and at the same time as Ann Stalker. Mary tells of working from 4:00 a.m. until after 10:00 p.m. seven days a week providing food and bedding for anywhere from thirty five to one hundred fifteen men at a time. Every day she baked a loaf of bread per man, as many as thirty pies for the noon meal, tea cakes[58] for the evening meal, and biscuits or pancakes for breakfast. At times she used a barrel of flour per day. Yeast had to be made fresh each day in a five

---

[55] Whayne, *A New Plantation South*, 16.
[56] Anna Ritter, "Marked Tree from 1883-1936," in special issue, *Marked Tree Tribune*, (July 17, 1939), 24.
[57] Ayers, *Southern Crossing*, 8.
[58] In the southern United States, a teacake denoted a large dense cookie made with sugar, butter, eggs, flour, milk, and some sort of flavoring.

gallon churn crock.⁵⁹ Both the noon and evening meal also required meat and vegetables of some kind and the only leftovers that the men would tolerate was boardinghouse hash, a concoction of chopped beef roast, potatoes, onions, soup stock, salt, pepper, and sage, pressed into a pan and baked brown which they would sometimes serve for supper. While Mary and her sister did the cooking and baking, at least two others, usually teenagers from the neighborhood would be hired to wait tables and all would help with the dishes. Mary's first child literally died of neglect due to her overwork in the boardinghouse. ⁶⁰ Ann would have had Caroline to assist with the cooking, and probably relied on young Florence and even little Ella to assist with waiting tables and dishwashing. It is even possible that her sister Paralee assisted in the boardinghouse as her husband, Jasper had died in 1882 and the extra money would have helped in her home. Bedding would have been washed, hung out to dry, and ironed fairly regularly as well, adding to the workload. It was difficult work but it gave her the financial boost she needed to become a self-sufficient woman.

The town of Marked Tree lay just three miles to the north and the town of Deckerville was four miles to the south, so a depot was not really needed at the Stalker farm, but the gravel pit necessitated a loading area, so one was to be constructed.⁶¹ This led to a depot town in a location where the railroad had

---

[59] The yeast that she speaks of is sourdough, a biological leavening containing the *Lactobacillus* culture. It is made by incorporating a bit of dough called the mother, which is placed in a flour and water mix. This feeds the mother and causes it to increase. Each time the baker uses the starter they add more flour and water to the mother. The mother can last for years at room temperature this way and each mother will have its own distinct taste.

[60] Mary Hamilton, *Trials of the Earth: The Autobiography of Mary Hamilton* (Jackson: University Press of Mississippi, 1992), 16.

[61] Interestingly, the older and once thriving community of Deckerville would not survive at all. It was located at the Joe Drace farm on the Poinsett and Crittenden County line.

not envisioned one. Tyronza was a town born of happenstance. With the activity around the depot and Ann's boardinghouse providing a steady stream of traffic for any would-be merchants, a town was sure to develop. With the planned depot came another improvement, a post office. An ambitious young man named Wesley Beatty applied to the postal department in 1888 for a post office to be housed within his small store, now fast becoming a bustling commercial establishment with the influx of railroad men and the people moving in to cut and mill the timber. The application asked that the station be named Beatty, after the aspiring postmaster, but the postal service rejected that name for whatever reason and assigned an alternate choice. Postal officials christened the small office Perkins, most likely after Ann Stalker's new son-in-law William Cornelius Perkins who had married daughter Caroline in 1881. Son Jimmy filed a homestead claim on the one hundred sixty acre parcel just south of Ann on October 29, 1881 and according to federal policy was required to clear and improve the land to complete his homestead. He never fulfilled the contract. Jimmy died shortly before he was to be married, on Christmas Eve of 1881, of a fever. He was only twenty-four.

When the railway officially opened for business in 1883, the Kansas City, Springfield, and Memphis Railroad, as it was now called, named the depot, then just a platform, Tyronza Station after the nearby river. The dual names continued for some time as there was already a Tyronza post office in Cross County.[62] Beatty eventually sold his store to a group of young men who would go on to prominence in the area, and with the store went the post office. The three – Ernest Ritter, his brother, Louis A. Ritter, and their friend John A. Emrich – would launch the firm of Ritter and Emrich with Ernest Ritter

---

[62] This Tyronza stood along what is now US Highway 64 at the Cross and Crittenden County line, just east of Parkin, on the banks of the Tyronza River.

receiving the postmaster's commission. When the other Tyronza went out of service, the three enterprising men jumped at the chance to clear up the confusion and applied for a new name. On April 9, 1888 the post office at Tyronza, Arkansas, entered into operation.

Tyronza was born of the railroad, created only because of the gravel pits. The railroad created a need for a town. Railroad towns were designed to be efficient and functional with streets laid out in a standard grid. Houses were built and stores followed and commerce soon became the primary activity.[63] Towns are like business propositions with survival dependent on transportation. Then, the railroad was a town's lifeline. Development grew around Ann Stalker's boarding house, with Ann and her daughters selling off the farm a piece at a time to those who wanted in on the action in the emergent community.[64] Over the next fifteen years, Tyronza grew around them as a timber center and railroad town.

The so-called Gay Nineties were good to the little town and to Ann Stalker. Her three daughters all married and established homes in the surrounding area. She fulfilled the homestead requirements on Jimmy's quarter section which bordered her land on the south and doubled her acreage.[65] Caroline's first husband, William Perkins died a couple of

---

[63] Joseph A. Amato, *Rethinking Home: A Case for Writing Local History* (Berkeley: University of California Press, 2002), 45.

[64] Ann, Ella, and son-in-law John Thorp platted the J.E. Thorp Addition to the Original Town of Tyronza shortly after he and Ella married. Until her death in 1903, Ann made almost monthly trips to Harrisburg to record land transactions.

[65] Jimmy's quarter section provided over forty bushels of corn and 1400 pounds of seed cotton in 1888 on only twenty cleared acres. It is plausible to expect an equal output on her own farm. The cotton seed money would surely have added to her income and the corn to her food supply and animal feed. She also reported having twenty head of cattle and ten hogs. See Martha Ann Stalker, Testimony of Claimant to fulfill the Homestead Application for The Heirs of James Baker, 25 August, 1888, General Land Office, Bureau of Land Management, National Archives, Washington, DC.

days after Christmas, 1888 just three days after she had given birth to their third child. She remarried a little over a year later to Marcus Aurelius Howard who remembered in a 1939 interview with his grandson Roger Howard that he came to Tyronza in 1889 because he had heard from his childhood friend Tom Hudson, that a man could find work there. When he arrived Tyronza consisted of a store, post office, a platform for a depot, a sawmill, and a cotton gin that was so small that the cotton was compressed by a man stamping it down with his feet. He not only found work, but through his best friend Tom Hudson, would also find a wife. Tom had married Florence Stalker and they introduced him to her older sister. He would marry Caroline the following January, the couple riding off together on the same horse to the Crittenden County seat in Marion, because they could not get across the swampy terrain to go to the Poinsett County seat in Harrisburg. They lived in Caroline's house, a half mile up the tracks from Ann in a pecan grove, and that is where they stayed until 1903 when Ann died. Caroline wanted a better education for her children than the little school in Tyronza could provide and in 1902 sent her three older sons to Cave City to attend a private academy.[66] Her aunt Paralee had remarried after Jasper's death to Squire Wilkins, and they had moved to Cave City. The boys stayed with her. Caroline refused to leave as long as her mother was alive.

Martha Ann Lewis Baker Pittman Stalker died in the month of October in 1903. At her death she was still living in her house on the mound, engaged in raising her young grandson, Jesse Hudson, who had been orphaned with the deaths of her daughter Florence and her husband Tom. One of her granddaughters remembered the long funeral procession crossing the railroad tracks to take Ann's body for her burial in the little graveyard at nearby Whitton in Mississippi

---

[66] Tyronza at the time operated a single one room school house for white children only.

County because Tyronza had yet to acquire a cemetery of its own.[67] She was sixty-eight years old. Sadly, she lies today in an unmarked grave.

Caroline and Marc moved almost immediately to Cave City to be with the boys and place the other children in school taking her nephew Jesse with them. They held onto Caroline's portion of Ann's farm as well as the land at Tyronza she had purchased with her first husband, William Cornelius Perkins, for several years with Marc either renting the farm out or returning during the growing season to operate it himself. He finally sold the place about 1912 to local businessman and banker John A. Emrich for $64.00 an acre, a healthy profit over the $2.50 an acre that Duncan and Ann paid originally. Two of the Perkins grandsons came back and opened a general merchandise store downtown around 1913 before finally selling out and moving to the area around Black Oak to farm. A few descendants are still in Tyronza today.

It is exciting to think about what Ann and her girls must have gone through, living out there on that mound in the swamp. She held onto her own quarter section of land as well as successfully claiming the quarter section that Jimmy had homesteaded before his death. She also fulfilled the homestead claim on an eighty acre parcel of land that Tom and Florence had filed, securing it for young Jesse. Although she never earned the right to vote, she prospered because she owned her land. Arkansas's very liberal land laws allowed her to own property and finally control her own destiny. The coming of the railroad not only opened up the country, it opened up a new life for a woman who had seen so much heartache. She not only survived but thrived, living out her

---

[67] I have yet to understand why Ann was not buried on the nearby Indian Mound that apparently held the graves of Duncan and possibly even Jimmy. Caroline's first husband was interred at Whitton, then called Dead Timber Cemetery, and she may have wanted her mother near him, especially since Duncan was not her father. It also brings Ann's relationship with Duncan into question as one of need rather than real affection.

life through one of the most tumultuous periods in American history. Although she never sought the title, above all, Ann deserves to be called the Founding Mother of Tyronza.

Chapter Three
Little Town in the Delta

Gain! Gain! Gain! Gain! Gain! is the beginning, the middle, and the end, the alpha and omega of the founders of American towns.

> *Morris Birkbeck,*
> Notes on a Journey in
> America *(1818)*

The commercial timber business in Poinsett County was made possible by the railroad, but heavy cutting began as early as 1880 in advance of the tracks. Railroad camps soon turned into logging camps and sawmills were built at depot towns. Oliver Davis came to Tyronza in the mid-1880s and established a large sawmill alongside the depot, employing several timber cutters and sawmill workers. He constructed a separate mill at nearby Marked Tree which he sold to the large Chapman and Dewey operation in 1890.[68] His son-in-law, William Beasley, learned the timber business from Davis and eventually operated his own mill up the tracks on the north bank of the Tyronza at Beasley Spur. Beasley added value to his lumber by hauling some of it to Tyronza where he built a cooperage, known to most as the box factory, and employed several workers. He constructed a logging railroad, or "dummy line" from the edge of town to Marlin's Swamp. A dummy line operated on tracks built of steel or wood, laid atop ties which were often no more than logs laid on top of the muddy ground. A small engine pulled a couple of cars back

---

[68] Gerald T. Hanson and Carl Moneyhon, *Historical Atlas of Arkansas,* (Norman: University of Oklahoma Press, 1981), 15.

and forth. The tracks could easily be pulled up when needed and moved elsewhere.[69] The timber company business was structured much like the plantation enterprises that followed on its heels. Workers were paid in company money or scrip known as doodlum, which was redeemable only at the company store. Everything a worker needed, he or his family purchased at that store.[70] As late as 1910 there were still two timber camp stores in operation in Tyronza Township.[71]

Like most railroad towns, Tyronza grew along the tracks with the depot sitting in the honored spot in the center. It acted as the gateway with visitors entering and leaving through its doors. All freight either coming or going ended up at the depot. The telegraph, the town's connection to the greater world, was maintained at the depot.[72] In Tyronza it was the way the newspaper arrived each day from Memphis. Each morning people would crowd the platform waiting for a salesman to come off the train to sell them their daily *Commercial Appeal* or *Press-Semitar*.[73] Main Street was created to run perpendicular to the tracks running between the depot and the combination store and post office. New merchants moved to Tyronza, staying in a boarding house until they had established themselves and could rent or build a home of their own. Many of the houses and businesses were built on stilts in

---

[69] George Beley, Field Notes, Personal Interview with the author, May 2010; and, Teddy Prestidge, Field Notes, Personal Interview with the author, Feb 25, 2008. See also, Tony Howe, "Arkansas Logging Railroads," Logging Railroads of North America, <http://www.loggingrailroads.com/ar.htm> (accessed February 23, 2012). Beasley's line was the Tyronza Lumber and Cooperage Co. line and ran for 2.5 miles. It was dismantled before 1907.
[70] Whayne, *A New Plantation South*, 27.
[71] *Thirteenth Census of the United States, (1910) Tyronza Township, Poinsett County, Arkansas.*
[72] John A. Jakle, *The American Small Town: Twentieth Century Place Images,* (Hamden, CT: Archon Books, 1982), 16.
[73] Clay East, Interview by Sue Thrasher. Tape recording, September 22, 1973 Southern Historical Collection, University of North Carolina, Chapel Hill, NC.

the early days to keep them dry from the overflow. Three men were employed full time in the township building those new homes.[74] Tyronza, with its slightly higher ground was not as susceptible to flooding as a town like Marked Tree, but it was not immune either.[75] Streets in the early years were often muddy pits that acted much like quicksand. An early resident tells of a mule that bogged down in the mud on Main Street around 1910, and had to be killed in order to free it.[76]

Among the early settlers in the area were two young Iowa natives, brothers named Louis and Ernst Ritter. Ernst would maintain his home in neighboring Marked Tree, but Louis would live in Tyronza. A youthful John Emrich came to Poinsett County in 1887 from his home in Kentucky. He arrived at Marked Tree on a raft of logs bound for the shingle mill there which was owned by F.G. Markart and Oliver Davis.[77] He stayed on and began work as a timber cutter for the two, settling first in Marked Tree. His son John tells in a 1983 interview that his father arrived in Marked Tree in October with sixteen dollars in his pocket. He was not paid until the following August and although he had gone for ten months without wages, he still had six of the original sixteen dollars. Timber cutters earned good wages, at least $1.00 per day, but the work was dangerous. Emrich recognized the need for merchants in the bustling little towns and with a bent for self-preservation, moved to Tyronza shortly after. Along with the Ritter brothers, they built the little store that they had

---

[74] *Thirteenth Census of the United States, (1910) Tyronza Township, Poinsett County, Arkansas.*
[75] East, Interview.
[76] Ibid.
[77] Markart was the maternal uncle of Ernest and Louis Ritter and lived in Leavenworth, Kansas where he managed the large and successful A.J. Angel & Company lumber business. Ernest Ritter had lived in Kansas and worked for him prior to his arrival in Poinsett County.

purchased from Wesley Beatty into a large, first class firm on Main Street just across from the depot.[78]

As the town grew along the tracks and gained respectability, families who demanded such civilized institutions as schools and churches began following the men to Tyronza. Weary of living in the wilderness and wanting better for her children and grandchildren, Ann Stalker donated a two-acre parcel of land to the Freewill Baptists for the purpose of constructing a church in the little village. It was located at the end of the growing commercial district, about three blocks from the railroad tracks on the land that her son Jimmy had started to homestead before his death. The large frame building served all the various denominations for many years, with each group taking turns hosting the services.[79] Ann may also have donated the land for the first school in town since that lot was also a part of Jimmy's homestead. The building stood across the street from the present elementary school, in the place on which the Church of Christ now stands. Frances Annie Howard Robards, a granddaughter of Ann Stalker, recalled that school in the early years in Tyronza held a split term opening three months in the winter and three months in the summer because the roads were too bad to get there in the fall and spring. She told of her father hitching four mules to the wagon to get through the mud to get her and her siblings to school at times.[80] *The Modern News*, the newspaper printed in the county seat of Harrisburg reported in its June 14, 1895, edition that Tyronza "is one of the most refined towns in the county. It has a few stores, hotel, church, schoolhouse, mills, gins and many other advantages and conveniences. It is

---

[78] Family legend states that Emrich secretly operated E. Ritter's liquor business as Mrs. Ritter was a prohibitionist.
[79] Teddy Prestidge, Field notes, interview with the author, Tyronza, AR, February 25, 2008.
[80] Howard, *Descendants of David Anthony Pittman*, 112.

located in the eastern part of the county and has a fine farming country, which is rapidly being developed."[81]

By 1900, Little River Township had been divided into three separate smaller political divisions, with newly formed Tyronza Township now encompassing the southern one-third of the original. It included not only the village of Tyronza, but the older town of Deckerville which sat along the railroad about four miles to the south. The population of the township stood at 800 and that included all of the people who resided in both towns as well as the surrounding countryside. 343 of those people lived at Deckerville, leaving 457 either in the town of Tyronza or living in the country between. Of that 457 people, 89 percent were white. Fifty-six percent were male and 44 percent female which is fairly evenly distributed considering that in neighboring Marked Tree, which had incorporated in 1895, there were very few women at the time with the majority of the men being transient mill workers. It appears that Tyronza residents were determined early on to establish a permanent town with families instead of a work camp. Eleven percent of the township's population was black, the majority of those being men who worked in the timber industry.[82] While Marked Tree sat in the midst of Chapman and Dewey's one hundred thousand acre holdings, land around Tyronza was held in smaller parcels and by more people.[83] These families owned between forty and two hundred acres with the farm work being done by the family and maybe a hired hand or two. Each family was responsible for clearing their own land of timber which they would then bring in to Oliver Davis for sale. Two large sawmills were constructed about a mile and a half from Tyronza at a place

---

[81] Poinsett County Historical Society, *Poinsett County, Arkansas: History and Families,* (Paducah, KY: Turner Publishing Company, 1998), 37.
[82] *Twelfth Census of the United States, (1900) Tyronza Township, Poinsett County, Arkansas.* All census data was transcribed into Microsoft Excel databases for analysis by the author.
[83] Whayne, *A New Plantation South,* 18.

called Dewey's Mill, operating until about 1912 when the good timber played out.

Clearing this land was no easy business. The soil was excellent and vegetation grew thick and lush. The forests of sweet gum, cypress, oak, and poplar were choked with river cane and underbrush. The larger trees would be cut and hauled to Tyronza for resale but there remained other trees that were deemed worthless by the timber buyers that had to be cleared in order to begin farming. This was accomplished by "deadening" the trees. A ring was cut around the base of the tree using an axe, which allowed it to die. After a couple of years the remaining tree was usually burned. While waiting for the trees to die, the thick undergrowth, as well as the tangle of roots from trees already removed, would be "grubbed out" with a hoe and the thick stands of cane would be burned. Once the land was clear of undergrowth and the larger trees, planting could commence around the stumps. The first season corn was usually planted, followed by cotton the second year.[84]

By 1910 the majority of people in Tyronza Township were engaged in farming. Although Tyronza was not yet incorporated, best estimates show the population at approximately 225 persons, with equal numbers of males and females. More than one-half of the population was under the age of twenty-five. Children under the age of eighteen numbered 102 while there was only one person in the town over the age of seventy, the venerable Oliver Davis. Slightly over one-half of the people were natives of Arkansas with the majority of the rest coming from neighboring Tennessee, Kentucky, and Missouri following in that order. At this time there was only one African-American living in Tyronza, a seventeen-year-old widow named Lizzie Harris who worked

---

[84] Otto, *The Final Frontiers, 1880-1930: Settling the Southern Bottom Lands.* (Westport, CT: Greenwood Press, 1999), 25, and Davies, "Introduction", 4.

as a cook for the Carl and Mamie Dysart family. Mr. Dysart had a good job as an inspector for the lumber company and most likely young Lizzie's late husband had been the unfortunate victim of a logging accident. By this time, Oliver Davis had sold his sawmill and gone into farming. He lived in Tyronza with his second wife and their housekeeper and was engaged in the real estate business, possibly selling plots of land that had been abandoned once the timber was removed.[85]

The landscape on the outskirts of Tyronza was looking much different with farms replacing the forests. The population of rural Tyronza Township in 1910 was 1,450. Although Tyronza was almost completely white, the African American population in the region had increased significantly as sawmills opened. While whites were employed by the lumber companies in great numbers, it was the black workers who performed the majority of the truly dangerous work in the timber.[86] Farming was already taking a lead in importance in the area. In 1910, 272 heads of household identified themselves as farmers', 60 percent of them were white. Of that total, 54 percent identified themselves as owning their farm, with blacks holding a slight edge in ownership. Approximately 41 percent of the population in the rural area was black, up from 11 percent just ten years earlier. Men still outnumbered women but only slightly making up 54 percent of the population and the gap was closing. The only area with a significantly larger male population was that centered on the two rural sawmills.[87]

Living conditions in a logging camp as well as in newly cleared farm land were difficult and the makeup of the

---

[85] *Thirteenth Census of the United States, (1910) Tyronza Township, Poinsett County, Arkansas.*
[86] East, Interview.
[87] *Thirteenth Census of the United States, (1910) Tyronza Township, Poinsett County, Arkansas.* Of the total farms in the township, 54.4% were owner operated. Of that total, 55% of black farmers owned their farm while 54.1% of whites were listed as owners.

households reflects that. Rural homes generally had both a husband and wife who had living with them their biological children, step-children, adopted children, nieces and nephews, cousins, siblings, in-laws, parents, grandparents, aunts and uncles, and wards of the court. It was not unusual for several children to be orphaned and to be "taken in" by various relatives if they had them, and neighbors if they did not. Women and men lost spouses at an alarming rate with the men generally dying in work-related accidents and the women succumbing to childbirth and exhaustion. Forty-seven percent of the total population of Tyronza Township, 791 out of a total 1677, was eighteen or younger in 1910, with one-tenth of those children under the age of one. One-third of these children were listed in the census as black or mulatto. For all of these children there were only two schoolteachers. Both of them were white.[88]

It can be assumed that the black children had no public school at this time, or if they did, it was barely functional. The State of Arkansas has long had a dismal record when it comes to educating its children, black or white. The Northwest Ordinance of 1787 established the practice of setting aside the sixteenth section of land in every township to use to maintain the public schools. In 1803, Congress enacted laws providing for the sale of all lands south of the State of Tennessee, and made provision for the reservation of section sixteen in every township for the support of public schools.[89] Arkansas gained possession of section sixteen lands when it became a territory in 1819, totaling over nine hundred twenty eight thousand acres. In 1843, the legislature created the Common Schools Act

---

[88] Ibid. Since the school at Tyronza was a one room affair, the other teacher most likely served the Deckerville school. The two districts merged before 1930 as the population moved toward Tyronza and Deckerville began its descent.

[89] The original town of Tyronza, encompassing one square mile or 640 acres, lay in the east half of Section 17 and the west half of Section 16, one of the sections set aside for schools.

which made provisions to lease or sell this land and place the proceeds in a perpetual fund to support public education. In land rich Arkansas, there was little incentive to lease land and much of what was sold was never paid for, which resulted in limited funds for the schools. After the Civil War, Arkansas's reconstruction governor, Isaac Murphy, a former schoolteacher, pushed for strong support for public education, including schools for black children. This was reversed during the era known as "The Redemption" and Jim Crow produced further discrepancy between the races. By 1900, it was estimated that less than 43 percent of Arkansas's school-age children were attending classes and the average school term was sixty-nine days. Arkansas had no "normal school" to train teachers until 1903, and until that time most of the state's teachers had no more than an eighth grade education. A 1921 federal education report stated, "...to be born in Arkansas is a misfortune and an injustice from which they will never recover and upon which they will look back with bitterness when plunged into adult life, into competition with the children born from other states."[90]

While conditions appeared bleak in the logging camps and small farmsteads, the residents of Tyronza seemed to be faring well. By 1910 the town could boast its own doctor, as well as an attorney. There were eight men engaged in the retail trade, with six of them in general merchandise and two running meat markets. Four other men were employed as clerks in these stores and one store, Ritter and Emrich, employed a full time bookkeeper. The town also boasted a restaurant, a blacksmith, a gunsmith, a locksmith, a sewing-machine salesman, two boarding houses and a photographer. John Emrich had expanded his enterprise by this time to include a bank, built next door to his general merchandise store and which employed a full-time cashier. He was already beginning

---

[90] Carl H. Moneyhon, *Arkansas and the New South, 1874-1929* (Fayetteville: The University of Arkansas Press, 1997) 75.

to amass the small tracts of land that eventually make him one of the most powerful businessmen-planters in the Delta.[91] At least three of the families were doing well enough to have domestic help living with them on a full-time basis.[92] The *Marked Tree Tribune* reported on July 25, 1911, that Ritter and Emrich had erected a $10,000 gin at Tyronza with six stands and an automatic press with a capacity of sixty bales.

Even though the timber industry had collapsed shortly after 1910, the richness of the bottomland soil harkened a new prosperity for Tyronza and its residents. Families flooded into the area from surrounding states to try their hand at commercial farming. As America industrialized, the country became less rural with people giving up the more difficult, but reliable subsistence style of farming. As commercial goods were mass produced and became more affordable, Americans from all walks of life desired to own them. While subsistence farming allowed a farmer and his family to survive, their purchases were limited in many ways by what they could barter for locally. Many people turned toward the money crops such as cotton and rice to earn a paycheck that would buy the items they desired. Thousands continued flooding into the Great Plains to break the sod and try their hand at growing wheat. Others went farther west to develop fruit and vegetable farms, but the Arkansas Delta was the land of cotton, and cotton was the crop that so many were determined to make their fortune with. Like so many who had tried before them, the odds were not that good.

As the timber companies cleared the land, many realized the value of the soil, but soil that is under water a large part of the year is not much good for farming. In order for the land to be viable it had to be drained of standing water and the annual

---

[91] Whayne, *A New Plantation South,* 150.; and Anna Ritter, "Marked Tree from 1883-1936" *Marked Tree Tribune*, July 17, 1939, 27.
[92] *Thirteenth Census of the United States, (1910) Tyronza Township, Poinsett County, Arkansas.*

overflows from the rivers controlled. The federal government had created the Mississippi River Commission in 1879 to encourage levee building along the river using past flood heights as gauges for future construction, but there also existed a desperate need for drainage in the region. In counties like neighboring Mississippi, to the east, only ten percent of the land was either in cultivation or in a condition that it could be cultivated. In 1893, residents of the Delta lands in Crittenden, Cross, Lee, Mississippi, Phillips, Poinsett, and St. Francis counties joined together to create the St. Francis Levee District. The district successfully pulled the water from the land and prevented the annual flooding that interfered with planting. Even with the success there was trouble. The timber companies had found ways to bring their crops out of the swamps without drainage and wanted no part of the taxes that were imposed on the landowners to construct and maintain the levees. As well, larger landowners who had purchased the more easily cultivated land early on did not wish to be subject to the taxes on their property that would benefit the smaller farmers and possibly their competition in the market. After drainage, thousands of acres of land that had formerly been under water and not surveyed became tillable. Large Delta landowners like Ernest Ritter, R.E. Lee Wilson, and Chapmen and Dewey Lumber Company, claimed the land that bordered their land based on riparian rights. After a series of court cases and a reversal of policy by the U.S. Department of the Interior, the newly drained land was deemed the property of the United States government and was opened for homesteading in 1908. Thousands of settlers poured into the region to join those who had long squatted in the Sunk Lands. Large landowners fought the decision while attempting to intimidate the homesteaders. These new settlers formed a Homesteaders Union to fight back in 1913, primarily to deal with Ernest Ritter and Lee Wilson. Local courts refused to let homesteaders cut timber on the disputed land, while the landowners reportedly paid vigilantes to burn them out. This made it difficult for the homesteaders to make good on their claim. The federal courts ultimately sided against the large landowners in 1922, but by that time most of the homesteaders had given up. In the eight years following the 1922 decision, E. Ritter and Company increased its Poinsett County holdings from 3,989 to 5,001 acres with only forty-six acres of the newly acquired lands outside the disputed area.[93]

While many of the timber companies, such as Marked Tree's Chapmen and Dewey, began farming their own land utilizing the help of tenant farmers, they had no long-term plans to become plantation owners. As the timber started to play out these companies would start to shut down their massive operations, selling their company houses, company stores and the land which usually went for bargain prices. Many small parcels were snapped up by newcomers to the Delta, who saw their opportunity for riches in the black soil. But cotton seed was expensive and in a land devoted so extensively to a cash crop, there was little in the way of wild or native plants to gather to feed the family, and any land used for food production was land that was not devoted to cotton and cotton was where the money was. In order to get these families started, merchants and cotton factors[94] utilized a

---

[93] Otto, *The Final Frontier*, 24. For a more detailed description of the Sunk Lands Controversy, see Jeannie M. Whayne. "The Power of the Plantation Model: The Sunk Lands Controversy." *Forest and Conservation History* 37, no. 2 (Apr 1993): 56-67.

[94] According to the Memphis Cotton Exchange, the cotton factor referred to a special kind of agent who served the planter as banker, broker and wholesale grocer. His importance increased after the Civil War. The factors' greatest years of influence were about 1870 to 1920. The factor often gave payment on cotton consigned to him before sale, with fixed interest rates charged. He received a commission of generally 2-1/2 per cent for selling the cotton. Because of the wide and varied service provided by the factor there were numerous possibilities for controversy and friction. In many ways, the local merchants were tied to the cotton factor much like the tenant farmer was tied to the merchant.

"furnish" system in which the farmer received his seed and the means to support his family throughout the growing season in return for a lien on his land. If the crop was good, the farmer paid off the lien, lived through the winter on his excess earnings, and started over again in the spring. Many times though the crop was not good. Heavy rains in the spring might prevent the seed from being planted soon enough which reduced the growth and restricted production. Some years the rain might wash the seed out of the ground requiring another loan for more seed and the possibility of a reduced crop. Still other years, no rain came at all and the fertile soil with its dense gumbo quality would dry up and crack taking the crop with it.

Floods like the one in 1913 left widespread devastation for months. That spring the Mississippi crested at forty-three feet above flood stage. This would have a devastating effect on the economic system in and around Tyronza. The *Tribune* reported on April 25, 1913, that water was finally on the decline after the April 11th levee break at Wilson but that water still covered the St. Francis basin over a forty mile radius east to west and a thirty mile radius north to south. Other years the crops would be damaged by serious droughts, and later insects like the boll weevil and army worm would devastate the fields. The furnishing merchant might carry a farmer through a couple of years of adverse conditions, but these men were entrepreneurs. Often barely staying solvent themselves, they could not continue to carry that much debt for long periods of time. Foreclosure on a crop lien meant that the land was forfeited to the merchant for the debt owed. The farmer usually was allowed to continue living on the land and farming as a tenant, hoping that he could eventually reclaim his property, which was rarely the case. While there were excellent years with outstanding yields, they might be followed by two or three disastrous ones in which farmers had nothing to show for their labor. Even in the years when there were no disasters, the market could play havoc with their margin of profit. A tiny change in the economy could spell disaster for the farmer.[95] Arkansas was a hard place in the early part of the twentieth century, and it would only get harder.

As war broke out in Europe in August 1914, the people of Tyronza persisted in building their town and pursuing their dreams. The town continued to prosper as more and more people flowed into the region looking for cheap land and the opportunity to make it big. President Woodrow Wilson was unrelenting in his pursuit of isolationism for the country and most Americans supported him. Germany's resumption of unrestricted submarine warfare in the North Atlantic and an attempt to entice Mexico into an alliance against the United States caused Wilson to change his mind. On April 6, 1917, Congress issued a Declaration of War and people in the United States began gearing up for a new challenge. In July a draft was instituted. According to the *Marked Tree Tribune*, Poinsett County was ordered to furnish 244 young men for the front. Of that first group, eighteen were called into service from Tyronza.

The American Red Cross was placed in charge of building morale and support for the war by requiring every community in America to participate in such activities as Liberty Loan drives. Because many had been against the war in the beginning there was a good deal of grumbling across the country when the United States entered it. In order to curtail the resistance, people were encouraged to report to the government those in their community, maybe even in their families, who were not supportive of the war. Communities were encouraged to compete against each other in fund raising, with those who failed to meet their goals being made to appear less patriotic than the rest. The editor of the *Marked Tree Tribune* encouraged other communities to follow the

---

[95] Ayers, *Southern Crossing*, 26.

example of residents of nearby Trumann in the northest corner of Poinsett County. There the townspeople got so caught up in the patriotic fervor that town fathers publicly whipped two men who refused to support the Liberty Loan drive. They then proceeded to the business of a merchant who had failed to contribute his full share. While the ladies of the town painted the front of his store yellow, the men took him out on the street and whipped him. They afterward decided to round up all of the town's "loose women" who were summarily thrown in the overflow by the men.[96] The ladies then pulled the hapless women out of the water and applied the lash to them. They then marched the whole lot downtown to the depot, put them on the train and ordered them never to return. The same issue of the newspaper reported that Tyronza had exceeded expectations in its first loan drive by collecting over $17,000 among the citizens, and with no mention of public floggings. The Red Cross called out the women of Tyronza and asked them to do their part to help supply the troops with the items they would need at the front and in the hospitals by forming knitting leagues. The woman answered the call and by the end of their first day, the thirty-five women assembled were able to ship to a central collection site at Marked Tree a total of thirty-five sweaters, thirty pairs of socks, seventeen wristlets, sixteen helmets, twenty-seven pairs of bed socks, twenty operating gowns, forty-four hospital shirts, twenty suits of

---

[96] The overflow is an annual affair in the Delta region, although some years it is larger and more significant than others. The levelness of the land resulted in slow drainage of the rivers. In the spring, when the rains come, the rivers and ditches swell and either top the levees or breach them. The water rises slowly and stays for weeks sometimes, before it drains off leaving a layer of sediment everywhere. Before the construction of the larger levees and the attempt to control the Mississippi and its tributaries by the Corps of Engineers, the overflow was often a jolly affair, much like Mardi Gras, with much drinking and partying by residents who could no longer work in the fields or in their regular business. I have been told that the overflow site in Trumann was also the site of baptisms as well as prostitute dunking.

pajamas, eighty-two towels, forty-eight undershirts, and forty pairs of under drawers.

While the war heated up in Europe and more and more young men left the cotton fields around Tyronza, improvements were still being made, most likely spurred by the price of cotton. The *Tribune* reported on October 12, 1917, that cotton was at its highest price since the Civil War. That week William Potter of Lepanto had sold eight bales to J.K. Mitchell for $1,600. On June 28, 1918, the *Marked Tree Tribune* reported that Wood and Warren Dry Goods had finished installing electric lights in their building, while John Emrich was constructing a new storehouse at his building.[97] While the people of Tyronza had war on their minds, they continued to move solidly into the future.

In January of 1918, a severe case of the flu broke out among soldiers at an Army training facility in Kansas. Within days many young soldiers had died. Because the illness was so severe and had spread so quickly, it caught military health officials off guard. Soldiers were shipped to bases all over the country before anyone realized the severity of the situation. The disease spread from the military to the civilian population and within weeks the entire country was infected. The illness was particularly frightening in its speed. A healthy young man could be walking around one minute and be dead by the same time the following day. While influenza normally kills some of its victims each season, they tend to be the ones who are weakest, the very young and very old. This strain was different. Fatalities were far higher among young people in

---

[97] John Emrich's remaining partner, L.A. Ritter, left Tyronza for Jonesboro sometime between 1912 and 1916 to open an auto dealership. They sold their Ritter and Emrich store to the firm of Wood and Warren who operated a dry goods store there for many years. Emrich had purchased land from Ann Stalker some years earlier to build a house and operate a small farm and he constructed a new store there in front of his home which he operated until taking over the firm of Howard and Young and their Tyronza General Supply.

their prime with the greatest loss of life occurring for those between the ages of twenty-five and thirty.[98] Public health officers in many areas sent warnings to government officials about the severity of the cases and asked for assistance. Eight months after the initial outbreak the United State Public Health Service had still failed to respond because its director believed that a major response to influenza was unwarranted.[99] People were dying so quickly that there simply were not enough trained medical personnel to assist with them. Telegrams flooded out of Arkansas requesting help with medications, nurses, and in the rural areas, doctors. It appears that in many parts of the state, white doctors were working with white patients first and letting the blacks go untreated. Urgent requests went out for "colored doctors" to come into the area and help. The results went unheeded, not because there was no one who cared but because no one else could be spared from any other town or county or state. The disease spread across the nation like wildfire. The visible symptoms were so frightening to those who encountered them that people refused to go near the sick. Individuals even refused to help their own family members, they were so afraid of the illness. Victims would bleed profusely from every orifice, even

---

[98] John M. Barry, *The Great Influenza: The Epic Story of the Deadliest Plague in History*, (New York: Penguin Books, 2005), 408. The story of the Spanish Flu Pandemic is a fascinating and frightening one. Barry's book explains that the reason for the high death toll among those generally considered the most able to fend off an attack was that the victim's own immune system fought so hard to stave off the disease that they died of something called a cytokine storm. Normally when a pathogen invades the body, the immune system sends cells to fight them which are activated by cytokines which stimulate the pathogens to produce more cytokines. This feedback loop continues until the pathogen is defeated. In the 1918 flu season, the pathogen may have mutated slightly resulting in too many cytokines being produced in certain parts of the body which eventually will kill. The cytokine storm seemed to focus on the lungs in this pandemic causing them to fill up completely with tissue so the patient could no longer breathe.
[99] Ibid, 309.

their eyes. The buildup of fluids and tissue in victims' lungs as their bodies fought to kill the disease resulted in cyanosis which caused their skin to turn a dark grey; some were even reported by doctors to turn a brilliant shade of indigo before they died.

Without acknowledgment by the President or public health officials and with the push to service the war effort, communities continued to gather to support the war effort, allowing the disease to spread.[100] An infected woman, who might feel fine when she left home, could carry the disease to every woman in a Red Cross knitting league. They, in turn, would carry the disease to their families. No one community in the country was spared including Tyronza. The flu took two young members of the landowning Prestige family within a couple of weeks of each other. It took John Emrich's young and popular wife Rose, just two weeks after giving birth to another son, leaving five children without a mother.[101] People died so fast that there were not enough caskets to bury them in. Headstone carvers ran out of granite and other stone so they made makeshift markers of cast concrete. Several of these markers dot the cemetery at Tyronza as well as the African American cemetery across the road surrounding Cherry Beam Church. Many more graves went unmarked.[102] There is no way to know how many actually died of the flu as many were too poor or too sick to call for a doctor and died without the

---

[100] Ibid, 308.

[101] Prestidge, interview field notes.

[102] While graves go unmarked for a variety of reasons, lack of funds, desire, or of someone left to remember the deceased, there were times during the pandemic that the situation was so severe that normal community function broke down. Teresa Parker of nearby Whitehall in Poinsett County reports that there are a number of flu markers in the town that were bound for one of the other communities in the state bearing the same name (there are four communities bearing the name White Hall or Whitehall in Arkansas). The situation was so severe at the time they arrived that no one would or could take the effort to determine where they should have gone, and they remain there until this day.

death ever being recorded. Even in the best of times local newspapers tended to make note only of the deaths of the influential in their pages and blacks were not noted at all unless the death occurred in some spectacular manner such as homicide or suicide. The federal government's request for local newspapers not to report flu deaths, so as not to arouse fear, only makes this information that much more difficult to collect. It appears that the *Marked Tree Tribune* followed the government's request and failed to note the cause of death in the obituaries that it actually ran. It is only from oral tradition that it is possible to learn the cause of death. All the while, the war raged on.

Before the flu had even settled down, the war was over. For millions of African Americans who had been called into service, the war had bought them a new sense of fairness and freedom that they had never before experienced, but brought home the reality that even though they were fighting to help the United States make the world "safe for democracy" they were still not treated with equality at home. Also angry were millions of immigrant workers in the northeast, as well as native-born coal miners in the mountains of West Virginia and Kentucky and cotton mill workers in places like Alabama and the Carolinas. The war had opened their eyes and many realized that their situation at home was bad. While political ideologies such as communism and socialism were known before the war, especially in places like the Delta, events like the Bolshevik Revolution brought them to the forefront, and fear of such armed uprisings spread throughout the nation in what has since been termed the Red Summer of 1919. While union organizing and strikes were mounting in the east, conditions in the Delta would only grow worse. On September 30, 1919, a small group of black sharecroppers gathered at the Hoop Spur Church north of Elaine in Phillips County for the purposes of organizing a union to protect their interests in their dealings with white planters. Their meeting was raided by a group of Phillips County lawmen and a firefight ensued.[103] White residents of the majority black Phillips County stated that they feared for their lives. Women and children were put on a train for Helena for safety and an armed mob of whites swarmed into the community. Within twenty-four hours the governor of Arkansas arrived with the United States Army in tow. What actually transpired after their arrival has never been proven, but whites refer to the event as a riot while blacks refer to it as a massacre.[104] Though the event cooled union passions among Arkansas sharecroppers for a time, Tyronza was on a collision course for an uprising of its own.

---

[103] Raided is not exactly an appropriate word, but the intent was the same. The officers, accompanied by an African American jail trustee, stopped a few yards short of the church and exited their vehicle. To this day, no one knows who fired first but the church was reported to have been riddled with bullets. It was burned within twenty-four hours of the gun battle so no evidence remained.
[104] Grif Stockley, *Blood in their Eyes: The Elaine Race Massacre of 1919*. (Fayetteville: University of Arkansas Press, 2001), xiii. Both Stockley's work and Robert Whitaker's more recent work, *On the Laps of Gods: The Red Summer of 1919 and the Struggle for Justice that Remade a Nation*. New York: Crown Publishers, 2008, provide an excellent look at the state of racial affairs in both Arkansas and the nation at the time.

Chapter 4
Boom, Bust, and Trouble

The times were dreadful, but it was just how it was, and we got very used to it. That was our civilization. The valley of the shadow. And it might as well have been Ur of the Chaldees for all people know about it now.

Marilynne Robinson
Gilead *(2004)*

Before the war brought normal life to a halt and the flu brought death to so many, a real estate developer named William H. "Coin" Harvey[105] retreated to the Ozark Mountains of Arkansas and built a million dollar resort community on the White River called Monte Ne. The place was beautiful and

---

[105] William Hope "Coin" Harvey was an American lawyer, real estate developer, mine owner, and politician. Born in what is now West Virginia in 1851, Harvey began a law practice in Ohio, later moving to Chicago. He moved his family to Ouray, Colorado, and operated a silver mine successfully until the price of silver fell to disastrous levels. He moved to Pueblo, Colorado, and entered into real estate development, before moving to Ogden, Utah, where he promoted a carnival. He became interested in the free silver issue in the early 1890s and moved his family back to Chicago to work in support of it. He published a very successful book called *Coin's Financial School* in which a young financier named Coin argues the merits of free silver. It was from this publication that he obtained his nickname. In 1896, he campaigned for William Jennings Bryan and discovered the land in northwest Arkansas was full of economic potential. He moved there and began building Monte Ne near Rogers. The Ozark Trail, although promoted as a good roads campaign was essentially a way of promoting his resort. When the scheme failed, he withdrew to Monte Ne. In 1931 he entered politics again forming the Liberty Party because he felt the two major parties were one and the same. He was nominated by the party as their candidate for president in 1932. Harvey finished sixth overall in the election, garnering over fifty-two thousand votes. He died at Monte Ne in 1936 and was buried there.

many were drawn to its doors, but it was secluded and difficult to reach. Harvey initially created a railroad, the Monte Ne Railway Company, which suffered a series of economic setbacks and finally with the coming of the First World War was abandoned. Thanks to Henry Ford, the automobile was in mass production, and more and more Americans began working for wages because they wanted to make owning a car a reality. Harvey concluded that if a series of paved roadways were constructed, the business brought to towns by tourists in cars would be unparalleled. This was a part of a movement that was spreading across the nation called the "Good Roads Movement" and it would take the country by storm. In 1913, Harvey created an organization called the Ozark Trails Association to encourage the construction of paved highways across the country. The Ozark Trail's main route ran from St. Louis to Tucumcari, New Mexico. It would later become the base road for the famed Route 66. Harvey proposed a spur route extending from Springfield, Missouri, to Monte Ne in Benton County, Arkansas. Enthusiasm for the project grew and additional spurs were created by boosters in towns across the country. One of those spurs was conceived between Springfield, Missouri and Memphis, Tennessee, paralleling the St. Louis and San Francisco Railroad, more commonly known as the Frisco Line, which had bought out the Kansas City, Fort Scott, and Memphis Railroad in 1903.[106] City fathers in Memphis were working feverishly to finish construction on the Harahan Bridge, which in addition to carrying rail traffic over the Mississippi River, would also carry two auto lanes, one

---

[106] John Solomon Otto, *The Final Frontiers, 1880-1930: Settling the Southern Bottom Lands.* (Westport, CT: Greenwood Press, 1999), 63.

suspended on each side of the railroad bridge from Arkansas into Memphis.[107]

City fathers from Jonesboro to West Memphis joined together in a series of meetings to discuss the benefits of joining the movement. It was decided that the construction would be done in sections with promoters in each of the towns providing the capital for the project. The businessmen of Tyronza joined forces with neighboring Marked Tree and agreed to pave a ten-mile-long section from the St. Francis River Bridge in Marked Tree to the Crittenden County line south of Deckerville.[108] It would utilize the newly constructed Tyronza River Bridge that had been built by Tyronza and Marked Tree residents and finished in May, 1917.

A three-man board to oversee construction and let contracts was assembled whose members were Ernest (E.) Ritter of Marked Tree, and John A. Emrich, and Dewey D. White of Tyronza. Former Tyronza resident Louis A. Ritter, Ernest's brother and John Emrich's business partner, won the contract to build the road which was to be constructed according to Ozark Trail specifications.[109] Made of concrete, the roadbed was twenty feet wide, with twenty-one foot tall identical obelisks placed in the center of the roadway at the town limits. These markers were lighted and included distances to larger cities, and all were to include the distance to Monte Ne. Identical white signs with the letters "OT" in green were placed at intervals along the roadway. Since the Marked Tree to Tyronza section was completed after the demise of the Ozark Trails Association it is not known whether these

---

[107] "Good Roads in Arkansas," *Christian Science Monitor*, (July 23, 1913): 13,; and Nan M. Lawler, "The Ozark Trails Association," (master's thesis, University of Arkansas, 1991), 11.

[108] Ritter, "Marked Tree from 1883-1936," *Marked Tree Tribune*, July 17, 1939, 26.

[109] Jeannie M. Whayne, *A New Plantation South: Land, Labor, and Federal Favor in Twentieth-Century Arkansas*, (Charlottesville: University of Virginia Press, 1996), 138.

markers were ever constructed in the area. Since they were to be placed in the center of a twenty foot wide highway, only a small handful survive across the country, and it is doubtful that the one at Tyronza would have survived long if it was erected at all.

The road through Tyronza came down alongside the railroad tracks between Ann Stalker's old house and the original store and post office, then made a ninety degree turn to the south at the depot in order to avoid that structure as well as Oliver Davis's old sawmill. It made another ninety degree turn to the east approximately four blocks away, just past the Tyronza General Supply store on what is now Mullins Street, and rejoined its previous course along the railroad tracks a few blocks later. The roadway along the tracks in town was planted with stately American elms, then a popular choice for such avenues as they provided an attractive and welcoming view as well as a cooling shade for travelers.[110] Vaughn Clanton, a Tyronza bridge builder, saw the potential of the new roadway and constructed a handsome new service station across from the depot in Tyronza, in the spot where Wesley Beatty's first store had stood, to service the cars that inevitably would be traveling along the route. Tyronza with its location halfway between the Crowley's Ridge town of Jonesboro, home of one of the state's new agricultural schools, and the lively river port at Memphis was a perfect stopping point and the town was ready to welcome travelers.[111] Unfortunately, Coin Harvey died and his Ozark Trails

---

[110] Prestidge, Field Notes, Personal Interview with the author, Feb 25, 2008. In 1928, Dutch elm disease arrived in the United States and began spreading across the country. By 1950, over one-half of the nation's trees had been lost to the disease. It appears that most of Tyronza's original trees are still standing between the old highway and the railroad tracks apparently spared the ravages of the disease due to the fact that so few trees remained in the region at the time that the disease never gained a foothold.

[111] Clay East, Interview by Sue Thrasher. Tape recording, September 22, 1973 Southern Historical Collection, University of North Carolina, Chapel Hill, NC.

Association folded up just as the Tyronza portion of the road was finished, so the towns in that section were never placed in the official guidebook. Nevertheless, the highway would have a tremendous impact on the landscape and the people of Tyronza for years to come.

The 1920s brought much change to Tyronza. The nation celebrated the end of the war and a general sense of prosperity, and many of its citizens gambled on first one business adventure after another. Many became almost obscenely wealthy. People built bigger homes, bought fancier cars, drank to excess (even though the Twentieth Amendment had made it all illegal), and lived their lives as if there were no tomorrow. On April 24, 1925, the Tyronza correspondent to the *Marked Tree Tribune* reported a "building boom" in Tyronza with four new "bricks" nearing completion. These buildings constituted what is known as the Grossman Block and anchored the section of Main Street operated by Jewish merchants. Escaping severe persecution in Russia and Eastern Europe, the rural American South of the early twentieth century provided a safe haven and an opportunity to forge a new life for many Jewish families. Frank Grossman opened his store in Tyronza in 1925 with the financial assistance of his brother, Joiner merchant Jack Grossman. Also operating stores on the block were Jacob Speil, Harry Sokol, and the Evensky family.[112] These families would remain an important part of the social fabric of Tyronza for many years.

Agriculture, on the other hand, was not feeling the effects of the upswing. A postwar recession that began in 1919 and lasted until 1926 saw record low prices for cotton. The price of cotton lint fell from thirty-two cents a pound to thirteen cents a pound. Cotton seed fell from sixty-six dollars a ton to twenty-two dollars a ton. The value of land fell dramatically. Farmers responded to the crisis in the only way they knew

---

[112] Beley, George. Interview with the author, March 16, 2010.

how, they planted more cotton.¹¹³ The year 1921 saw the first wave of boll weevils to hit the state, which had long been free of the insect.¹¹⁴ Farmer after farmer lost their land to the furnishing merchants and those who had already fallen into tenancy in previous years fell even farther, moving into the ranks of the sharecropper. Farming was already firmly entrenched in the economic system in Tyronza Township and the census records show signs of the miserable situation that lay ahead. Economic conditions in the latter part of the nineteenth century had gone against small landowners. Large numbers of landless whites now joined a formerly majority black group of tenants and sharecroppers. Of the 272 heads of household in 1920 that were engaged in farming, only seventeen owned their own land. Fully 67 percent of Poinsett County farmers were tenants by this time.¹¹⁵ Events over the next twenty years would render the situation even worse, with the owners falling into tenancy and the renters falling further down the ladder into sharecropping.¹¹⁶ By 1930 fully 78 percent of Poinsett County farmers would be sharecroppers; another 2 percent were tenant farmers.¹¹⁷

The larger landowners, like John Emrich, not only survived this slump, but came out of it better off than they had been before. As a furnishing merchant he increased his holdings

---

¹¹³ Otto, *The Final Frontier*, 57.
¹¹⁴ Ibid, 65.
¹¹⁵ Gerald T. Hanson and and Carl Moneyhon, *Historical Atlas of Arkansas*, (Norman: University of Oklahoma Press, 1981), 124.
¹¹⁶ Tenancy, although falling a step higher on the socio-economic scale in the eyes of Delta citizens, was really no more than sharecropping. Tenants usually owned their own equipment, such as a plow and a mule, whereas sharecroppers had to rent these items from the landowner. This allowed a tenant to receive a larger share of the crop at the harvest. While a sharecropper could usually expect no more than 50 percent of the crop he had raised, a tenant was allowed to get as much as 70 percent.
¹¹⁷ Based on data obtained from the University of Virginia Library's Historical Census Browser located online at <http://mapserver.lib.virginia.edu/>.

substantially during the decline. Tenant farming was based on the crop lien system which was basically a mortgage on the future crop. In return the tenant family was given a line of credit at either a bank or a store that was to be used to purchase supplies to get the family by until the crop came in. Many families managed the loan well and purchased only the basic necessities, but others spent freely, placing themselves in jeopardy of not being able to pay out of the loan at ginning time. In bad years even those who were frugal had trouble paying off their note. The system was broken no matter how good or bad the crop was. Noted Southern historian C. Vann Woodward, himself an Arkansas native from Vanndale in neighboring Cross County, described the crop lien in his seminal work *Origins of the New South* by saying that the tenant "...pledged an unplanted crop to pay a loan of unstipulated amount at a rate of interest to be determined by the creditor." A major shift in ownership occurred during the decade of the twenties with the number of individual landowners decreasing in southeastern Poinsett County by 6.7 percent and the number of sharecroppers increasing by 14.3 percent.[118] Nationally sharecropping had always been thought of as a black problem, but by 1935 white sharecroppers outnumbered blacks by a two to one margin. The ranks of new sharecropping families increased during the 1920s at a rate of 40,000 each year.[119] This decade saw an exodus out of the Delta by black farmers, long at the bottom of the social and economic ladder in Arkansas. Their ranks decreased statewide by three percent between 1920 and 1930.[120] All the while those in town continued to prosper, building new homes and

---

[118] Whayne, *A New Plantation South,* 142.
[119] Holley, Donald, *Uncle Sam's Farmers: The New Deal Communities in the Lower Mississippi Valley.* (Urbana: University of Illinois Press, 1975), 7.
[120] Otto, *The Final Frontier,* 73.

businesses, and creating ill will among those in the rural areas who had less and were falling further behind.

In the early spring of 1926, forty-five male citizens of the community met to submit a petition to incorporate the Town of Tyronza to the County Court of Poinsett County. Every business and professional man in the town signed the document, including William Beasley, now grown old and grey and known affectionately as Uncle Billy, with one very notable exception. Banker and planter John A. Emrich's name was not on the petition. Why? It seems that even if he were out of town for business or pleasure, or busy with some project, that the rest of the group would have waited for his signature. They did not and one can only assume that he was not supportive of the move. Again, why? What did he stand to lose by the move for incorporation? The petition was submitted by the esteemed town attorney, Aaron McMullen, who had been a settler for almost as long as Beasley. On May 17, 1926, Articles of Incorporation were filed in the Secretary of State's office in Little Rock. Tyronza was now officially a town. The *Marked Tree Tribune* reported that on September 10, 1926, the town held its first election with 109 votes cast. The citizens elected businessman and bridge builder Vaughn Clanton as their first mayor. H.D. Price was elected recorder with Albert Fair, W.M. Howard, T.F. Lillard, L.M. Wood and interestingly, John A. Emrich elected aldermen. Postal clerk Roy Howell was named the town's first law enforcement officer.

The women of Tyronza were busy improving the city as well, raising the money to purchase two and one-half acres of land adjoining the old Webber Cemetery[121] just south of town, from planter Hiram Norcross, to establish a city cemetery and provide a fund for perpetual maintenance. On October 20,

---

[121] The Webber Cemetery, like the East Cemetery closer to town, was on an Indian mound. It is still visible in the back corner of the city cemetery, though most of its markers have broken and fallen into disrepair.

1926, the Tyronza correspondent to the *Marked Tree Tribune* bragged, "Our little village is noisy. Our electric light plant beats away every hour of the twenty four. Our two gins have already ginned 2,087 bales of cotton. Wagons and trucks get in as early as 3 o'clock and the gins have closed as late as 12."[122] A week later she reported that at one time the preceding Saturday over one thousand persons had been on Main Street. She pleaded with the newly elected city officials to mark lines on the street to prevent someone being killed by a car while trying to cross it.

By this time, the single church in town that had been built on land provided for such a purpose by Ann Stalker was filled to overflowing each week, but in a state of serious disrepair. After a tongue lashing from a traveling minister who contrasted the sad and disrespectful state of Tyronza's single church building to the cleanliness of the town, the progressiveness of its business community, and the excellence of the school, the various denominations that worshipped there decided to go out on their own and construct their own buildings. The Baptists were first with the Baptist Women's Missionary Society raising money for construction by selling hamburgers and Coca-Colas every Saturday morning to the throngs of people coming into town from the countryside. They sat up their stand under the branches of a large chinaberry tree on Main Street across the street from the current church building.[123] Their large attractive yellow brick building was dedicated on January 20, 1928, at a cost of $25,000. The Methodists followed shortly afterward with their own brick building behind the older church structure, complete with stained glass windows that had been purchased by individual family members at a cost of $75 each.[124] The other denominations also erected their own buildings and the

---

[122] Tyronza Items, *Marked Tree Tribune*, October 20, 1926, 5.
[123] Prestidge, interview field notes.
[124] Poinsett County Historical Society, 39.

old community church was eventually torn down, a victim of progress. A city park was established on the location.

The late summer of 1926 saw unusually heavy precipitation in the central portion of the United States. The Mississippi River and its tributaries began rising on the upper stretches as early as September. The rain continued on through the autumn and into the winter. As the temperatures warmed and the winter snows began to melt in the North, the run-off combined with the incessant rain in the Midwest and South, bringing the rivers up to dangerous levels. The directors of the levee districts, afraid that residents on the opposite side of the river would dynamite the Arkansas levees in the hope of taking the pressure off of their side, placed armed guards on their banks. Twenty-four hours a day they patrolled the tops of the structures keeping a watchful eye on the massive earthen works, all the while their directors plotted ways to destroy the levees on the other side if the situation became necessary.[125]

Water backed up in the tributaries of the Mississippi and flooding began along the St. Francis and Tyronza rivers, running thousands out of their homes. Like the unanswered calls for help during the flu pandemic in 1918, pleas for assistance poured forth but there was no one available to come as a large part of the country was seized by the same conditions. The water levels fell once, but then more rain brought the rivers back up. When the waters finally receded in mid-summer, the devastation left behind was overwhelming. Many homes were washed away and those that remained were so coated with mud and debris that it was easier to tear them down and start over than try to clean them up. Although it was late in the season, the farmers planted their cotton but with little success. Very little cotton was ginned in 1927 and several more families fell by the wayside.

---

[125] John M. Barry, *Rising Tide: The Great Mississippi River Flood of 1927 and How It Changed America,* (New York: Touchstone Books, 1997), 192.

On October 29, 1929 Americans witnessed the crash of the New York Stock Exchange. Business plummeted all over the nation and even the wealthy suffered. Thousands of acres of Poinsett County farmland were lost to back taxes. To compound the problems, 1930 brought a new crisis throughout the South. After picking up the pieces from the '27 flood, the rain stopped. Beginning in the spring of 1930, over the next eighteen months no appreciable rain fell on Poinsett County. The harvest of 1930 ended with no cotton. Tenants couldn't pay the planter for their furnish. The planter couldn't pay the merchant or the bank. The merchants foreclosed on more and more crop liens amassing acres and acres of land that they couldn't pay the taxes on, and times grew worse. The financial panics earlier in the century had brought about the creation of the Federal Reserve in 1913 but the act only covered national banks. State banks and the thousands of local banks were on their own. Because local banks depended on one another to maintain the public's faith in the banking system, the failure of one was likely to bring a cascade of failures over a wide region. In Arkansas, over one hundred local banks failed.[126] The *Marked Tree Tribune* reported on Friday, November 21, 1930, that Monday had seen the closure of both the Bank of Harrisburg and the Bank of Lepanto. On Wednesday, J.A. Emrich's little Bank of Tyronza closed its doors as well. Devastated by the failure, Emrich promised his depositors that they would not lose their money. Accompanied by a group of Tyronza business and professional men, Emrich petitioned the bank examiners to allow him to be placed in receivership of the bank and pledged his personal fortune of $300,000 as security.[127]

---

[126] Otto, *The Final Frontier*, 85.
[127] Emrich's granddaughter, Judy Perry Black, recalled that the Emrich daughters went on a shopping spree in Memphis shortly after the bank failed purchasing a number of new clothes. When they arrived home with their purchases their father was livid and ordered all merchandise returned.

Although they had reservations, the request was granted. It is believed to be the only time in the state's history when an officer of a failed institution was allowed to do such a thing.[128] Emrich used the Bank of Marked Tree to hold the assets he was accumulating to repay the depositors, but lost everything he had achieved when that bank also failed and he was forced to start over. Before the decade was over every bank in the county, except the Bank of Trumann, would go under.

Rainfall amounts during the summer of 1931 were the lowest ever recorded in Arkansas.[129] Families across the country were starving, begging for assistance of any kind. The federal government led by President Herbert Hoover believed that people should and could take care of themselves, and refused to provide federal aid, believing instead that any assistance should come from the local or state level. Poor states like Arkansas had few resources to give to their people. The American Red Cross was called into service but following the same "up by your bootstraps" mentality, issued garden seed to 123,000 Arkansas families instead of food.[130] The people went home and planted the seed, but without rain, it would not even sprout. Only the turnips survived and many joked about eating a turnip sandwich which was a slice of turnip between two other slices of turnip.[131] The Red Cross finally realized how desperate people felt and began issuing food rations but even that would run into problems. When the Red Cross ran out of food vouchers in the little sharecropper town of England, in rural Pulaski County, Arkansas, and refused to issue the food that was allocated, hungry farmers rioted. Local

---

He reportedly told the girls that they would not be wearing new clothes while he owed all of those people money.
[128] "Appoint Bank President Agent" in *Wall Street Journal (1923 – Current file);* Nov 29, 1930; ProQuest Historical Newspapers: The Wall Street Journal (1889 -1993) pg. 6.
[129] Otto, *The Final Frontier,* 83.
[130] Ibid, 87.
[131] Ibid, 84.

merchants realized the severity of the situation and knowing that they would eventually be reimbursed, turned their stock over to the farmers. In Poinsett County, local planters controlled the Red Cross ration board and used the position to their advantage. In order for a family to receive a one dollar Red Cross food voucher[132] they had to work clearing and grubbing[133] plantation lands, an activity which should have paid two to three times that amount. Public outcry from people in the county ended the practice but the committees, fearing the sharecroppers would get used to what they called "rich food," gave only the plainest rations, such as cornmeal, flour and lard. The sharecroppers supplemented their meager diet with an occasional rabbit, which they referred to as a "Hoover Hog".[134] In 1933, after eighteen months of work, John Emrich finally accomplished the goal he had set out to achieve and paid back every depositor the full amount of money they had lost in the failure of the bank. Residents believed that the worst was over for Tyronza, but they could not have been more wrong.

Sometime in the late 1920's, a young man named Harry Leland Mitchell and his wife, Lyndell moved from their home near Halls, Tennessee, to Tyronza. Mitch, as he was called, had sharecropped in Tennessee while teaching in a little one-room schoolhouse for extra cash. The couple was encouraged by his parents to join the rest of the family in Tyronza, the father Jim, a barber in the town, bragging about the potential of the land for farming. Mitch arrived in Poinsett County set to sharecrop for the Brakensiek Brothers, but was immediately put off by the condition of the housing and facilities for

---

[132] The one dollar voucher was what was allocated for a month's worth of food for each person.
[133] Grubbing is the process of clearing land of the underbrush and roots left behind after timber clearing. Workers used a large, heavy hoe, called a grubbing hoe, to chop the underbrush down and then to work the roots out of the ground leaving soil that is ready to be planted.
[134] Ibid, 87.

sharecroppers in Arkansas. Mitch stated that the gravel road ended at the plantation commissary and that the little two-room sharecropper shacks sat close together down a muddy lane behind it. Cotton growing right up to the cabins, they had been built of green lumber and the shrinkage that came about from the normal drying of the lumber left large cracks between the boards in the walls and the floor.[135] He instead took over a little clothes press that lay unused in the back of his father's barber shop and set up shop as a dry cleaner. Mitch had for some time been a devout follower of Socialist teachings. His political leanings had at various times put him at odds with many of his neighbors, but he discovered in Tyronza a kindred spirit in an unlikely person.

Henry Clay East was born in Tyronza at the turn of the century to a large and prominent landowning family. While not in the wealthy planter class, the family was comfortable and greatly respected by almost everyone in the community. His grandparents, John Harston and Charlotte Montague East had come to Poinsett County from the area around Savannah, Tennessee at the end of the nineteenth century, bought land and established themselves as competent farmers. His father, Joseph Arch East, operated a successful grocery store and meat market located near the community church on Church Street. He also ran a small farm where he raised cattle for slaughter and resale in his meat market. Clay worked for his father doing a variety of jobs. One of his positions required him to sleep in the back of the store in town. Clay reported that someone had to stay at the store at all times in order to keep the merchandise from being stolen. Many times he shared his quarters with one or another hired men, usually carpenters from back east or immigrants from Europe who his father had hired to build barns or houses on the farm. It was

---

[135] H.L. Mitchell, *Mean Things Happening in this Land: The Life and Times of H.L. Mitchell, Cofounder of the Southern Tenant Farmers Union*, (Montclair, NJ: Allanheld, Osmun, 1979), 16.

from them that he first learned of labor unions, although at the time he reported that he was "strictly independent" and believed that everyone was capable of taking care of themselves.

After finishing school, Clay traveled around the country taking a variety of jobs, but eventually returned home to Tyronza. In 1922 he married Maxine Goodrich and shortly thereafter took a job working for her brother-in-law, Vaughn Clanton who was a bridge contractor and future mayor of Tyronza. Clanton got a job building a bridge back in the East family home of Savannah, Tennessee and Clay worked there for three years.[136] Clanton was interested in cars and with the Ozark Trail Highway, which shortly after its opening became Arkansas Highway A-7,[137] coming through Tyronza he wanted to get in on the action. His father fronted him enough money to build a new gas station at the first corner in Tyronza, which is now Main and Frisco Streets, and he offered Clay the opportunity to operate the station for him which Clay eventually purchased. Clay and Maxine purchased a house on the A-7 Highway, what is now Mullins Street in Tyronza. His only child, a son named Jack remembered that the house was his father's dream home, with a fenced back yard. He called the home his father's "lock, stock and barrel."[138] The gas station was located in the same building as Mitch's Tyronza Cleaners. While discussing ways to efficiently run their businesses, Mitchell discovered that Clay also had Socialist leanings, a matter that Clay at first strongly denied. An uneasy

---

[136] Clay noted in his interview with Sue Thrasher that the bridge was built over Indian Creek and was still in existence. A check of an historic bridge website, Bridgehunter.com, reveals that the bridge with its ten foot wide span is still open for vehicular traffic.

[137] The A-7 later was renumbered U.S. Highway 63 until being bypassed in the fifties. It is now Frisco Street, then becomes Main Street and later turns and becomes Mullins Street.

[138] Jack East, interview with Van Hawkins, Southern Tenant Farmers Museum Oral History Collection, 16.

friendship developed between the two in the spirit of reaching out to those who needed help. With a little encouragement from Mitch, Clay became an ardent Socialist and talked up his politics to everyone who came through the door of his business.

In 1931, Mitchell and a local tenant farmer named Alvin Nunnally received a charter for the first Socialist party chapter in the state of Arkansas. The Tyronza Socialist Party was born. Clay East was among the first to join, waiting until he had secured his election as Tyronza's city marshal. The two men organized political rallies in and around Tyronza, even hosting the Arkansas Socialist Party Convention in 1932, pitching a large circus-type tent on the athletic field behind Tyronza High School. The featured speaker at the event was the party's candidate for President of the United States, Norman Thomas. Interest in the organization was high with as many as 150 people showing up at the regularly scheduled meetings at the Odd Fellows Lodge hall on Main Street in Tyronza. The two would host political rallies in front of their businesses on a regular basis. Local residents called the corner of Frisco and Main Streets, where Clay and Mitch's businesses were located, Red Square to mock their political activity. The laughter would not last long.

Times were hard in Tyronza by the time the Socialist Party set up shop in the town in 1931. Farmer after farmer had lost his land and his equipment due to flood, the boll weevil, army worms, drought, non-payment of taxes, financial calamity, or some combination thereof. The merchants owned thousands of acres of rich farmland but they knew little about how to farm. They desperately needed the sharecroppers and tenants to keep the land in operation.[139] No one could pay for anything and even the bank had gone under so there was no credit immediately available for keeping things going. The local landowners gathered together to discuss their options. John

---

[139] Whayne, *A New Plantation South*, 5.

Emrich had been the furnishing merchant for most of Tyronza for several years, but the loss of the bank and the increasing demands of his accumulated lands were more than he could handle. He had even ended up with the farms and merchandise of one of his competitors, Mac Howard and Van Young, who had operated a general merchandise store across the street from Emrich's, in a loan default over back taxes. Together, the landowners went to visit Mallory Wholesale Grocery in Memphis to present an offer. They would jointly back each other financially to keep their operations afloat. Each man would operate his own plantation commissary as cheaply and efficiently as possible to try to keep their enterprises solvent and to hold the families that worked for them on the land.[140] While the local landowners tried desperately to hang on, it was the election of President Franklin D. Roosevelt that set in motion a series of events that would change Tyronza and its residents forever. Programs were started within weeks of his inauguration that promised to put America back on its feet again.

New Deal / Raw Deal

Among the relief programs was the Agricultural Adjustment Administration (AAA), which changed the way America farmed forever. The AAA's plow-up campaign was one of the most controversial aspects of the New Deal. It required farmers to destroy crops in the field as well as livestock in an effort to lower the supply to increase the demand. Delta planters and sharecroppers alike were required to plow up every third row of cotton in the field. They were to be compensated by a cash settlement to be dispersed as soon as the plow-up was completed. The checks were made out to the landowner who was supposed to provide the individual sharecroppers and tenant farmers with their share. Many of

---

[140] Prestidge, interview field notes.

the planters believing old bills should be settled up first, held on to the tenant farmers and sharecroppers share of the checks and applied the money to back debts. The planters said that sharecroppers and tenants had been known to leave a crop in the middle of the night to avoid settling up on a debt and many planters feared the same would happen again. The effectiveness of the AAA has long been debated. While many historians agree that it at least brought some hope to many parts of the country by putting cash into the hands of strapped farmers, there is no doubt that it favored the wealthy landowners over the landless.[141]

Mitchell and East watched as the local landowners took control of the county boards created to distribute the federal aid money, many manipulating it to their advantage. The sharecroppers and tenant farmers mostly went without and what was doled out to them came with a price attached, usually additional labor on one of the committee members' land in exchange for relief. Together, Mitchell and East rounded up their fellow Socialists as well as local businessmen who were not a part of the planter system and formed the Unemployed Citizens League of Tyronza to assist those who needed help. When a Civil Works Administration project was awarded to Tyronza to complete a new water system for the town, jobs were secured for local unemployed workers. The group had achieved their immediate goal and they disbanded.[142]

---

[141] For a good discussion of the Agricultural Adjustment Administration and its effects on southern sharecroppers, see Donald H. Grubbs, *Cry From the Cotton: The Southern Tenant Farmers Union and the New Deal,* (Fayetteville: University of Arkansas Press, 2000), pp. 17-22.

[142] Donald Grubbs, *Cry From the Cotton: The Southern Tenant Farmers' Union and the New Deal,* (Fayetteville: University of Arkansas Press, 2000), 28. See also, Jeannie Whayne, *A New Plantation South,* 188-92. Clay East in his 1973 interview with Sue Thrasher for the University of North Carolina's Southern Historical Collection did not remember the Unemployed League at all.

But Mitchell and East saw more problems. The two young men become convinced that the AAA was actually limiting farm employment and encouraging landowners to act in a dishonest fashion. When local Tyronza landowner Hiram Norcross relieved twenty-three families of their sharecrop and put their meager belongings out along the road, East and Mitchell set out to prove their assertions of so they could show them to the rest of the country. They sought the assistance of a University of Tennessee physiology professor and Socialist party leader from Memphis named William Amberson, who convinced Norman Thomas to fund the study. That study, published as a pamphlet under the title, *The Plight of the Share-Cropper*, proved their theory and even executives within the AAA itself agreed with the results. Thomas encouraged the pair to organize a union of sharecroppers and tenant farmers, not to take on the planters themselves because the tenants were too weak to accomplish that, but to put pressure on the AAA which was already divided on policy and procedure and could possibly be changed. East and Mitchell agreed, and rounded up a few friends from across the country to assist them with the launch. A war was about to be waged with Tyronza at the center of the fight.

Eye Openin' Time

On July 18, 1934, in a small dilapidated school house just south of Tyronza, eighteen men, seven black and eleven white, met together to create the Southern Tenant Farmers Union (STFU). In order to achieve their goal, the group organized interracially, installing an integrated slate of officers. All union locals were to be organized as interracial units which was a powerful force when dealing with local planters. They had usually utilized some sort of white supremacy to separate the poor underclass, but the STFU was to be different. At least for a time, the difficult economic situation prompted left-leaning whites and blacks to forget racial differences. The STFU helped two dozen of its members to file a lawsuit against planter Hiram Norcross. Norcross was accused of openly cheating and evicting tenants in 1934. The group lost the case in the Arkansas Supreme Court and appealed to the United States Supreme Court which decided in favor of Norcross. The AAA, set up by Secretary of Agriculture Henry Wallace, an Iowa corn farmer, had not taken into consideration the special situation that surrounded tenant farming and sharecropping and had not allowed this class of farmer to be considered in the distribution. Hiram Norcross had done nothing illegal, although his actions were not what the AAA had in mind. The ruling encouraged planters and they stepped up efforts against the STFU locally. Planters, overseers, and deputies threatened, beat, and reportedly killed STFU members and supporters, as well as evicting them from their homes.[143]

Over the next few months, East and Mitchell would help direct the activities of the fast-growing group from the back of their businesses in Tyronza. The union, though, was bad for business in the community. National media swarmed into town and reports of the conditions found on some of the local plantations cast a bad light on the region as a whole. A group of local men, many of them of the business class, formed groups of nightriders that patrolled the region striking fear in the sharecroppers. Both Mitchell and East feared for their lives but refused to be cowed by the actions of the vigilantes. When violence failed to work, the women of the town stepped up with their own response, an economic embargo. They began sending their clothes to Marked Tree for cleaning and stopped filling up their cars at East's gas station. Their husbands also paid off their debts to the two and moved their business

---

[143] Otto, *The Final Frontier*, 95. How much of this activity occurred in Tyronza Township is unclear. The majority of activity took place in the Poinsett, Cross, Crittenden, and Mississippi County area as that was the center of the union strength early on. Crittenden County landowners and officials seemed to be especially brutal in their treatment of union members.

elsewhere. This was more than Mitchell and East could handle. By 1935, they had both fled Tyronza for the safer confines of west Tennessee. Mitchell continued to run the union from a new office in Memphis, and East took over the operation of another gas station at Bartlett. Clay East was becoming increasingly uneasy with Mitchell's style of operation, fearing for the safety of not only himself but the membership in general, and would eventually cease his union work altogether. The union would continue to operate in other parts of the South taking root in seven different states and claiming to enroll as many as 40,000 members, but Tyronza's leading citizens had succeeded in rooting out what they deemed an undesirable element from their midst and things seemed to quiet down.[144]

---

[144] Interview with Henry Clay East by Sue Thrasher, Southern Historical Collection E-0003, September 22, 1973. The number 40,000 was supplied by H.L. Mitchell and was purely an estimate that many consider to be greatly exaggerated. The union operated rather loosely and membership records were sporadic at best. Many sharecroppers and tenant farmers never officially joined the union out of fear or lack of funds, but supported the organization as best they could.

Chapter 5
Memories and Conspiracies

They eat the same kind of food that we eat; they live in the same kind of shacks that we live in; they work for the same boss men that we work for; they hoe beside us in the fields; they drink out of the same bucket that we drink out of; ignorance is a kill'n' them just the same as it's kill'n' us. Why shouldn't they belong to the same union that we belong to?

Myrtle Terry Lawrence
Southern Tenant Farmers
Union organizer (1936)[145]

Arkansas is not known for its liberal politics even though most of the politicians have a (D) after their names when they show their pictures on television or when they get written up in the newspapers. The state's political leaders are what many Democrats call DINO's, meaning Democrat in Name Only, though there have been a few who espoused a more progressive stance. The state held on to its Democrat moniker in the 1950s, rather than going Dixiecrat and later Republican like the rest of the south, when Arkansas's young and idealistic governor, Sid McMath, became the only southern governor to support President Truman when he integrated the military. The Democrat label stuck, but the politics really went the way of Strom Thurmond and later Trent Lott and Ronald Reagan. That being said there were several alternative movements in the early twentieth century which included the

---

[145] Elizabeth Anne Payne, "The lady was a sharecropper," in *Southern Cultures* 4:2 (Summer 1998): 7. *Project MUSE*. Web. Accessed 11 June, 2011.

Populists, Agricultural Wheel, and the Socialist Party. While they failed to overthrow the Democrats they served the discontented elements in the state and gave them a platform of their own. The Socialist Party in Arkansas, along with Louisiana, Texas, and Oklahoma, was one of the strongest in the nation and had a fairly large following in the state prior to World War I. In 1912 Eugene V. Debs received over 80,000 votes from those four states in his bid for the presidency.[146] While the party virtually died in the state during the First World War, it sparked again in the Delta in the thirties.

The story of the Southern Tenant Farmers Union and its connection to the town of Tyronza is difficult to sort out. The best known story comes from H.L. Mitchell, whose telling of it makes the union sound as if it were a sort of populist uprising coming from the sharecroppers themselves and that he and Clay East just happened to be at the right place and at the right time to be involved. They were then joined by a variety of young militants who heard about the union struggle and made their way to Tyronza to join. The truth may be a bit more complex and could explain at least some of the hostility toward the union from its inception.

Mitchell's socialist ideas were swirling in his head long before he came to Tyronza. He was already reading the Little

---

[146] G. Gregory Kiser. "The Socialist Party in Arkansas, 1900-1912," *The Arkansas Historical Quarterly* 40 (Summer1981): 119-153. This article is a fascinating look at the Socialist Party in the state in the early part of the twentieth century. While most of the activity of the party occurred in the Little Rock area and the western half of the state where party leaders were attempting to unionize coal miners, there were at least three newspapers in the Delta region that supported the Socialist cause. They were the *Critic* in Piggott, the *Revolutionist* in Jonesboro, and the *Monroe County Socialist* in Clarendon. One of the early adherents to the party was a Madison County farmer named Sam Faubus, who named his three sons for Socialist Party heroes. One of those sons, Orval Eugene Faubus (named for Eugene V. Debs) later attained notoriety as the Governor of Arkansas during the Little Rock Central High School desegregation crisis.

Blue Books[147] and supporting third party politicians[148] while still a teenager in Halls, Tennessee. Arriving in Arkansas in 1927, his political ideas met with no warmer a reception from the establishment in Tyronza then they had back in Tennessee. It was the eventual recruitment of Clay East that really brought his activity to the forefront because Clay could get away with more in the town due to his family background. Their creation of the Socialist Party local in 1932, in collaboration with a local tenant farmer named Alvin Nunnally, brought them in contact with like-minded people from across the state and the nation. That organization had already brought future union organizers like J.R. Butler, Claude and Joyce Williams, and Ward Rodgers to town to meet and discuss ways to organize the sharecroppers, originally for the Socialist Party and later at Norman Thomas's suggestion for a union.

Mitch also had already met Socialists Howard Kester, William Amberson, and Willie Sue Blagden long before their work on behalf of the union. In May, 1933, Mitch left Tyronza to attend the Constitutional Convention for Economic Reconstruction in Washington, DC. His first stop was in Memphis where he met Dr. Amberson and Blagden, who were already active members of the Socialist Party, for the first time. Mitchell and Blagden, who would later gain fame as the white socialite who was beaten by a group of businessmen and riding bosses near Earle, Arkansas and whose bruised thighs would grace the front page of newspapers across the nation,

---

[147] The Little Blue Books are repeatedly mentioned in oral histories with Mitch and Clay. They were a series of 3½ x 5 inch, stapled, paper bound books published by the Halderman-Julius Publishing Company of Girard, Kansas. Emanual Halderman-Julius was a publisher and journalist who moved to Girard to work on the Socialist newspaper, *An Appeal to Reason*. He eventually bought the company and began printing the Little Blue Books as a way to put great literary works in the hands of the masses.

[148] He handed out flyers in support of Progressive Party candidate Robert M. LaFollette, Sr. in 1924.

rode on together to Nashville where they spent the night at the home of Howard and Alice Kester.[149]

Howard Kester was only twenty-nine at the time, but was already a veteran of the class and race war and his ideology had transformed from his non-violent beginnings as a theology student at Vanderbilt Divinity School, where he studied under J. Alva Thomas, to a radical and militant stance. So militant in fact that he had been removed as a board member from the Fellowship of Reconciliation (FOR) because he refused to change his opinion on the use of force between strikers and management which FOR believed was too aggressive. He joined the militant wing of the Socialist Party which advocated violent class struggle and wanted to turn it into a "militant working class party." He had been denied a spot on the board of directors of the NAACP because he had gotten "too radical."[150] He had also been denied ordination by the Cumberland Presbyterian Church due to his increasingly aggressive stance on social and racial issues. His wife, Alice supported his work and in fact had been a member of the Socialist Party in advance of her husband.[151]

Mitch traveled on to the convention where he was first exposed to the idea of racial equality and integration. He said later that he believed until that time that each race had its

---

[149] Blagden and Claude Williams made the trip from Memphis to Earle to investigate the alleged lynching of union member Frank Weems. Weems was taken into the river bottoms and beaten, but survived his ordeal. He managed to escape the area and got himself to Chicago where he surfaced weeks later. It was the photos of Blagden's bruised body and the fact that the planters had assaulted a white woman that propelled the STFU into a national story. She and Williams would recreate their roles for the March of Time newsreel, *Land of Cotton*.

[150] Anthony P. Dunbar, *Against the Grain: Southern Radicals and Prophets, 1929-1959,* (Charlottesville: University of Virginia Press, 1981), 62.

[151] Robert F. Martin, *Howard Kester and the Struggle for Social Justice in the South, 1904-1977.* Charlottesville: University of Virginia Press, 44. Howard and Alice differed on their interpretation of socialism with Alice believing that it was less a political ideology than the "religion of Jesus called by a different name."

place and they should maintain those places, but a problem arose when the hotel hosting the conference refused to admit some of the speakers and conference goers because they were black and that opened his eyes to a new issue.[152] While at the conference he also met for the first time Socialist leader Norman Thomas and became one of his active supporters.

A few months later, Mitchell and East were working together on what they called an Unemployed Citizens League in Tyronza, dealing with labor issues on New Deal projects in the county. They were visited by Socialist Party organizers, Edward and Martha Johnson, who were both impressed with the two young men's zeal for their work. Martha Johnson wrote Norman Thomas and asked him to visit Tyronza to witness the work of the two among the poor of the Arkansas Delta. Martha Johnson told Thomas that in Arkansas were the "true proletariat" and describing the local sharecroppers as "inarticulate men moving toward revolution."[153]

Thomas made the decision to stop in Tyronza during his Southern swing in early 1934. The speaking trip was designed to combat the rise in popularity of Huey Long of Louisiana, who Thomas believed was a fascist in the making. Mitchell and East arranged for Thomas to appear at Tyronza High School and estimated a crowd approaching five hundred turned out to hear him speak. Prior to his speech the two

---

[152] This also created problems at home when Mitch started picking up laundry for cleaning from black families in the area. He tells that he was approached by several of the white ladies in the town who expressed their displeasure at having their families clothing mixed with those of the "nigras". Mitch states that he told him that he had two tubs in the cleaners, one for whites and one for coloreds, whereas he actually had a tub for white clothes and a tub for colors. He claimed that his explanation settled their fears. See Mitchell, in *Mean Things Happening*.

[153] Dunbar, *Against the Grain,* 86.; James Thomas Gay, "Norman Thomas: Tribune of the Disenfranchised," *The Arkansas Historical Quarterly* 44 (Winter 1989), 333.; and M.S. Ventkaterami, "Norman Thomas, Arkansas Sharecroppers, and the Roosevelt Agricultural Policies, 1933-1937," *The Arkansas Historical Quarterly* 24: (Spring 1965), 8.

drove Thomas around the countryside to give him a firsthand look at the situation among the sharecroppers and tenant farmers of Poinsett County. Later at lunch in Clay and Maxine East's home, Thomas told the two that since the sharecroppers were disenfranchised based on the poll tax, the best way to organize them was not through socialism, as they couldn't vote anyway, but as a union.[154]

Mitchell wasted no time organizing the union. He sent out a call to interested parties to come to Tyronza for the purpose of organizing the sharecroppers. The meeting was held at the Socialist Party local's usual rented meeting space in the Odd Fellows Hall on Main Street.[155] Mitchell and East were present as was Uncle Charlie McCoy from Trumann, who had been a mentor to the two as they formed their group in Tyronza. John Russell Butler hitchhiked over from White County. Looking every inch a sharecropper with his craggy lined face and wild hair, J.R., as he preferred to be called, was a former schoolteacher who was working at his brother's saw mill to give him time for his Socialist Party work.[156]

Ward Rodgers came as well, bringing with him Joyce Williams. Rodgers was a Vanderbilt seminarian who had answered a call to a small Methodist congregation in the tiny west Arkansas coal mining community of Paris. His parishioners were so poor that he reached a point that he could not in good conscience take money from them and resigned his post, moving in with the Presbyterian minister and his wife. That couple happened to be another Vanderbilt

---

[154] Dunbar, *Against the Grain,* 87. See also, Mitchell, *Mean Things Happening in this Land*; and Grubbs, *Cry From the Cotton,* 29. In Mitchell's earlier work, *Roll the Union On: A Pictorial History of the Southern Tenant Farmers Union,* he does not mention Thomas or the Socialists in the formation of the union at all.

[155] The building still stands, a two story structure owned by the Upper Room Apostolic Church and sitting alongside their newly constructed church building.

[156] See Interview with J.R. Butler, Southern Historical Collection, University of North Carolina.

trained seminarian, Claude C. Williams and his wife, Joyce. They leaned toward Communism and had angered their congregation of businessmen and coal mine supervisors fairly soon after their arrival in the town by reaching out to the miners and the underclass in the community. Claude had gone into competition with the local pool hall by installing a pool table in the church and he and Joyce hosted the local young people to gatherings in their home where they discussed a variety of issues, including sex. They were in the process of building what they called a Proletarian Church and Labor Temple in tiny Paris, when the congregation stopped paying them and evicted them from the manse.

Mitchell had also written to Kester, imploring him to come as well. Arkansas has long been known as a backwater, and among the poor of the state there was little contact beyond their own communities. The planter class was another story. They traveled regularly and participated in fraternal organizations and business groups that took them throughout the nation and around the world. They were regular newspaper readers, not only of the local papers like the *Marked Tree Tribune* and *Osceola Times*, which covered the society columns and church and school news, but the *Commercial-Appeal*, covering the Memphis community, which many were closely tied to through their children's school and church activities. Tyronza at the time was still a fairly new town and although thought by the Poinsett County people as refined, it was not for people like the Norcross family who had come only recently from St. Louis. Hiram Norcross had been a railroad attorney who traveled in the highest circles of society. Religious life was limited as well and many traveled to Memphis to attend church or synagogue.[157] They also followed such newspapers as the *New York Times* and the *Atlanta Journal-Constitution* and they traveled in circles with people

---

[157] Tyronza had only four white churches at the time, Baptist, Methodist, Church of Christ, and Pentecostal.

from the larger cities. They were aware of radical activity in other parts of the country and throughout the South and many of these names, like Kester's, were well known. It is no wonder that the local power elite got their guard up early.

By the time Mitchell and East meet with the sharecroppers at Sunnyside Schoolhouse, the formation of the Southern Tenant Farmers Union was a foregone conclusion. East related in a 1973 interview about riding around Tyronza in his car while Mitchell explained the whole thing to East, Butler, and Ward Rodgers. It appears that all four were among the eleven white men who met to organize on July 13, 1934. Charles McCoy, a Trumann resident known by everyone as Uncle Charlie, was almost certainly there as he was one of the strongest members of the Socialist Party in the region and had attempted to organize a union years earlier at the Singer Company in Trumann, a move that cost him his job.[158] Mitchell had already decided that he was to be the secretary and that East would be the president before they ever arrived. While Mitchell tells only of sharecroppers like Ike Shaw and Alvin Nunnally speaking that night, East recalled that it was he who first spoke about the need for an integrated union and who signed up the first member.[159] Mitchell, Rodgers, and Butler met soon

---

[158] Mitch relates a particularly humorous incident concerning McCoy in his book, *Mean Things Happening in this Land: The Life and Times of H.L. Mitchell, Co-Founder of the Southern Tenant Farmers Union.* McCoy had an active Socialist Party local in Trumann in the early part of the twentieth century when Socialism was more prevalent in the state. At the same time, the Ku Klux Klan was also active in the state and the two sides clashed in an election for mayor of Trumann. The town was split fairly evenly, but McCoy and the Socialists did not trust the Klan to run a fair election and decided on some trickery of their own. At some point late in the evening, the Socialists cut the electricity to the building where the votes were being counted and during the ensuing melee, stuffed the ballot boxes which resulted in a Socialist victory.

[159] See Clay East Interview; J.R. Butler Interview; Mitchell, *Mean Things Happening*; Mitchell, *Roll the Union On,* 30. Clay says that he told Mitch from the beginning that he would act as president of the union for only one year. That seems to be supported by Mitch in a letter he wrote to Kester just

afterwards to draw up a constitution for the union and to apply for a charter to make the union a legal entity.

Teddy Prestidge, the son of Tyronza planter, James "Big Jim" Prestidge, has long insisted that Mitch was in the union business for the money. He tells time and time again that the union charged ten cents a month for dues from people who did not have anything to give. Anthony Dunbar in his conversations with both Mitch and J.R. Butler completed while doing research for his book, *Against the Grain: Southern Radicals and Prophets, 1927-1957*, states that both Mitch and Butler thought it could be a profitable venture. They had included a provision in the union by-laws allowing organizers to collect the sum of twenty-five cents for each new member recruited. Neither man apparently truly understood how destitute the sharecroppers they had planned to organize really were. The issue caused a rift between the two leaders that never healed. Butler never collected his organizing fees, which he blamed on Mitchell as the secretary and holder of the checkbook.[160] Mitchell never had the money to pay him because the sharecropper members often did not have the money for their dues and their immediate needs were often so overwhelming that the treasury was drained. STFU records are full of requests for food and clothing for families who were needy for one reason or another.

There has been much interest in Tyronza's response to the union, especially since the coming of the Southern Tenant Farmers Museum seemed to bring out a great deal of irritation among many of the townspeople. Attempts to gather

---

three weeks after the union formed in which Mitch said he was anxious for him to "come over here and see what Ward, Butler, and I have got started..."; see Dunbar, *Against the Grain,* 91.

[160] Interestingly enough, the Southern Tenant Farmers Union opened its first account in John Emrich's Bank of Tyronza. Clay East's wife, Maxine, herself an active worker in the union, served as the clerk there and signed the first deposit. See *Southern Tenant Farmers Union Papers, 1934-1977* (ProQuest).

information about people and events were met with responses that did not seem to match the story told by Mitchell. As a student working in the museum, I encountered anger and resentment aimed at me and my co-workers that seemed to point to a conspiracy of silence among the townspeople. No one could or would remember. Six years after I started, I am still not certain that I have an answer that satisfies me, but it is the only one that I can find. Tyronza was reported to be the most refined town in the county as early as 1896, only twelve years after the railroad resulted in its creation. Unlike the other Delta towns in the county, it was a railroad town rather than a timber company town and because of that seemed to have a larger number of families living there. Marked Tree and Trumann at the same time were wide open, hard-drinking, hard-fighting timber company towns with men outnumbering women two to one. Lepanto was no more than a logging camp built on a high spot in the swamp with the general store and post office maintained on a house boat for many years just to keep them high and dry. Tyronza was always different. It was a place for families, which is easy to quantify based on the equal numbers of men and women in the town as early as 1900 and the large number of children there. Forty-four percent of the population in 1900 was under the age of eighteen. By the end of the 1890s Ann Stalker had gone into business with her youngest daughter, Ella and son-in-law John Thorp, selling town lots for homes and businesses.[161] Maybe it was because the town's first real settler was a woman with four children (three of them girls) that Tyronza was more settled than the others. Whatever the cause, for better or worse, Tyronza was always different.

The problem with living in a small town is that everyone knows your business, whether you like it or not. In a previous

---

[161] The addition was known as J.E. Thorp's First Addition to the Town of Tyronza and included most of the downtown and the residential streets located immediately adjacent to it.

incarnation I worked as the director of the public library in a small town in southern Missouri. My assistant had been born, raised, and lived her entire life in the town and knew everyone there. If I needed to contact someone in town and could not reach them by telephone (these were the days before cell phones), all I had to do was ask Sally where they were and she could tell me. I remember one day needing to find one of the library board members to discuss an issue I needed an answer on fairly quickly. I couldn't reach her at home and I asked Sally if she had any idea how I might find her. She looked at her watch and said, "Well, it's 10:30 and it's Tuesday, so she will be at Donna's Beauty Shop getting her hair done. I'll give Donna a call." She called Donna and the board member was indeed there. I talked to her while she sat under the hair dryer. Tyronza is like that too. For many it is comforting to know that if you do not show up for your weekly wash and set, they will come looking for you. In a community like this there is no room for difference. It is just not accepted for long. I think this was the case with Mitchell and East and the townspeople. While the two and their political work might have been overlooked as long as it was just a local issue, they violated too many of the social norms by inviting outsiders like Kester into the town.

While the planter's response to the formation of the union seems extreme to us now, it is necessary to place yourself in their shoes to really understand their fears. Well known militant "Reds," as people like Claude Williams and Howard Kester were called, had invaded their home, promoting anarchy. The response by the planters intensified when at a December, 1934 union rally on the Main Street in Marked Tree, Ward Rodgers stated, "If I wanted to do so, I could lead a mob to lynch any planter in Poinsett County." Mitch, who had just arrived on the scene from a trip to Washington, DC, realized the seriousness of this statement and tried to deflect the outcome, but the damage had been done. One of Teddy

Prestidge's earliest statements to me about the union was, "Those people was gonna kill us. They said so." Even though many researchers, myself included, have always thought that his threat was an empty one made in the heat of the moment to rally the members, the more I learned about the radical element that came to help organize, the more I believe he may have been serious and the more I can understand the planters' fears.

One of the more interesting aspects of the union story is the juxtaposition of religious leaders in the struggle. Both Mitchell and East were atheists, but many in the leadership were ministers. Kester, Williams, and Rodgers were all Vanderbilt Divinity students who studied the Social Gospel under J. Alva Taylor during the twenties. Many of the black leaders were also ministers, although not formally trained, who led their locals like they led their flock, in search of the Promised Land. They were men like Arthur B. Brookins of Marked Tree who was an early supporter and organizer, and Owen Whitfield who led over one thousand displaced sharecroppers to camp along U.S. Highways 60 and 61 in Missouri so the people could "see what we're up against." Even the union's first lawyer, Virginia native C.T. Carpenter, had at one time been a minister, arriving in Marked Tree in 1910 to head the First Baptist Church. Without them the union never would have thrived.

On the other side were the other men of the cloth, like J. Abner Sage, who led the congregation at the United Methodist Church of Marked Tree. A former professor of hymnology at Emory University, Sage led a terrified opposition who saw the union as a threat to the entire community. Sage, known as "Brother" Sage, at one time hid in a boxcar to spy on a union meeting, and was quoted in a series of articles in *The New York Times* as saying that the sharecroppers are a "shiftless lot with only themselves to blame if they are not blessed with this world's goods as they would like to be." Sage also was angered by the union leaders' habit of addressing members, both black and white, as "Mister", and considered the union a "Red menace." He formed the Marked Tree Cooperative Association to counter the union influence among the business class in the town.[162] Looking through the lens of a modern set of eyes, Sage seems reactionary and narrow-minded, but how many of today's leaders, religious or otherwise, if faced with the same set of circumstances would respond in the same manner? It is a common practice to not make waves and attempt to calm emotions. While this may not be the ideal answer to a problem, it tends to be the practical one.

Teddy Prestidge tells how his father, Mr. Emrich, Mr. Norcross, and other planters in the community met and decided that the only way they could save everything was to go together to Memphis and put up everything they had to buy supplies to provide the furnish for the families that sharecropped for them. Without that, people would go hungry. He tells about coming home from school every other Thursday to help sack up pre-measured bags of beans, cornmeal, and coffee. They would weigh out pieces of pork side meat, and he would dip out buckets of lard from a fifty-five gallon drum until he was so greasy he could barely hold onto the dipper. All for the bi-weekly furnish that would be picked up by their tenants on Friday. His family's home and everything they owned was mortgaged to buy the supplies that kept the tenants from going without because the Prestidge's had no money either. As Prestidge puts it, "When you sacrificed everything you got, it gets under your skin just a little when they would join the union and talk the union talk."

---

[162] Interestingly, the worst of the violence aimed at the sharecroppers, at least openly, seemed to have come from Marked Tree rather than Tyronza and was targeted several times by national newspapers like *The New York Times* in articles that illustrated the violent response to the union.

The town, though, was made up of more than just planters and tenants. Most of the townspeople were businessmen, schoolteachers, and professionals. Their livelihood depended on taking care of both sides of those involved in the union fight. It is human nature to be jealous of those who have more than we do, and I am certain that there was at least some of that among the storekeepers and professional men caught up in the middle. There is also a tendency to look down on those who have less and place blame for their lot in life. I am certain there was some of that as well. I am also certain that many of these people felt helpless to do what they believed was right, and struggled mightily with decisions they had to make.

Teddy Prestidge says that among the mob of men who traveled to the union meeting in Birdsong in which Norman Thomas was pulled down from the stage and driven back to the Harahan Bridge with the order never to return to Arkansas was Tyronza mayor Bob Frazier. Clay East also tells that a few months later it was Mayor Bob Frazier who risked his own safety to drive to Bartlett, Tennessee to warn Clay not to come to Tyronza because there was a group of men who were planning to kill him. He said, "I don't know what they'd do to me if they found out I'd come over here and told you about this, but I just couldn't set there...I'd felt like I had your blood on my hands if I'd set there and not told you. But they're fixing to get you."[163]

One of the recurring comments visitors who grew up in Tyronza say when they visit the Southern Tenant Farmers Museum is that they had never heard of any of this. Jack East, Clay's son, who spent a couple of years of his life growing up in a house with the man partially responsible for the union and able to recall every building and business in the downtown business district after being away from the town for seventy years, related that he really did not remember any of it either. When asked whether he could recall anything

---

[163] Clay East Interview.

about the union and its creation he replied, "No, sir. I...'cause at the age of 10 years old that was the last thing on my mind."[164] If the child of the man responsible for the uproar does not remember anything about it, how are we to expect anyone else to recall it, and those children are the only ones left who can. Only a dwindling handful, like Teddy Prestidge who is now into his ninth decade, can recall what happened and even he was too young to truly know everything that occurred.

The Southern Tenant Farmers Union appears to not have been the spontaneous sharecropper revolt that Mitchell wanted it to be, and competing ideologies contributed to its decline in just a few short years. Most of the tenant farmers and sharecroppers who joined never got more for their trouble than more trouble. They were among the stragglers caught up in the last gasps of a system that was on its way out, and their lives would change with the rest of the world, for better or worse.

While people like Mitchell and Kester would publicly continue with their work toward social change, others like Clay East and J.R. Butler would go on with life, moving to new homes and jobs in faraway places. They still carried the ideas and the desire for change, and often worked behind the scenes to carry the movement forward. They would be joined by thousands of former STFU members who would move on to the far west to work in the factories or the fields, the upper Midwest to work in the auto plants, and the Deep South to take jobs in cotton mills and steel plants. The union would just

---

[164] Jack East, interview with Van Hawkins, Southern Tenant Farmers Museum Oral History Collection, 11. Jack East's mother was not a bystander in the union activity either. Maxine Goodrich East was apprehended by a group of Crittenden County riding bosses, along with STFU office manager Evelyn Smith Munro while attempting to photograph a group of union members who were being held and forced to work on a local planters land.

be another chapter in their lives that they pushed to the back of their mind as they struggled to make ends meet.

Many grandchildren of former union members have traveled to Tyronza to visit the museum that honors the struggles their ancestors went through to build a better life. Most of them knew nothing at all about their grandparents' work in the union until long after they were gone and one of the family members happened to come across a reference to their efforts. My great-aunt once told my mother that the reason she and her brothers and sisters did not talk about the Great Depression was because things were so bad and "we just wanted to forget." The sharecroppers, too, just wanted to forget.

Chapter 6
A New Generation Emerges

I have thought about that very often—how the times change, and the same words that carry a good many people into the howling wilderness in one generation are irksome and meaningless in the next."

Marilynne Robinson
Gilead (2004)

The latter half of the decade of the 1930s was quieter in Tyronza. With the union leaders out of their town, although not completely out of their lives, the place took on a more peaceful feel. The Tyronza news in the weekly *Marked Tree Tribune* was filled with the comings and goings of the planters and merchants, and sports and church events seemed to be the primary activities in the town.

In 1935 a high school coach in Nebraska, looking for a way for his tiny high school to play football in the lean Depression years, devised a game for a team of six players rather than the traditional eleven. The coach at Tyronza High School saw an article on the new game in the newspaper and proposed operating a similar league in northeast Arkansas that received national attention. Joining Tyronza in the new league were high school teams from Marion, Crawfordsville, Lepanto, and Turrell. The *Marked Tree Tribune* reported that on October 8, 1936 over one thousand fans filled the stands at Tyronza Stadium as the Chiefs took the field against the Lepanto Panthers in the first six-man game held under the storied Friday night lights. The Chiefs defeated the visitors by a score of 26-6.

Football was not the only sport that Tyronza residents followed. In 1935, about the same time that six-man football took the town by storm, during the height of the sharecropper problems, one of the local doctors, L.H. McDaniel, organized a baseball team for some of the town's young men. The games became so popular that the merchants and businessmen paid for the construction of a new baseball park at the edge of town to house the team in the midst of the Great Depression. Known as the Tyronza Independents they traveled over a three-state region playing at the semi-professional level. They were funded by a group of local businessmen and McDaniel, a former second baseman at the University of Tennessee Medical School, was known to be an excellent manager. His skills in coaching as well as recruiting and marketing made the games exciting. The games became so popular that all business in Tyronza would close on Wednesday afternoon so the townspeople could attend the mid-week event.

The year 1937 brought another crisis to Tyronza as well as a good deal of the eastern part of the United States — this one delivered by Mother Nature. Two large cold fronts stalled over the country in late December of 1936. One front hung over the western half of the nation covering the Upper Mississippi River Valley, while a second hovered over the south Atlantic. Tropical air masses that usually move to the east were forced north and northeast by these massive high pressure regions. The warm moist air mixed with the cold air over the Ohio and Mississippi Valleys and instead of falling as snow the precipitation came down as rain. The National Weather Service estimated over 165 million tons of rain fell on the region in January alone.[165] The excess moisture raised the water levels along the Ohio and Mississippi Rivers and their tributaries much as it had in 1927. The repair work along the

---

[165] American Red Cross, *The Ohio-Mississippi Valley Flood Disaster of 1937: Report of Relief Operations of the American Red Cross.* (Washington, DC: American Red Cross, 1938), 129.

levees after the 1927 flood prevented a repeat of the breaches that occurred in Mississippi. While good in some ways, the lack of a massive break anywhere in the levee system resulted in the tributaries not being able to release the excess water into the rapidly cresting Mississippi. The water in rivers like the White, the St. Francis, and the Tyronza had nowhere to go but up and eventually spilled out of their banks covering over 1.7 million acres of Arkansas land. Seventeen counties, including Poinsett, were under water.

Marked Tree received over twenty inches of rain in the first twenty-five days of 1937 while the temperatures dropped to as low as eighteen degrees. The January 28, 1937 issue of the *Marked Tree Tribune* reported that 87,000 Arkansas residents were now among the ranks of flood refugees and that the Poinsett County towns of Tyronza, Marked Tree, Trumann, Harrisburg, and Lepanto were housing a combined total of 8,000 refugees. The water on that day at Trumann reportedly rose at the rate of an inch every two hours and over five hundred people were housed in a temporary relief shelter at the Singer Community House. Tyronza with its higher ground had converted its high school into a refugee station and the little town of almost 600 residents was providing food, clothing, shelter, and medical attention for an estimated 600 flood victims.[166] The waters continued to rise and by the following week parts of town were underwater. Residents and the refugees they had been sheltering moved to boxcars on the railroad tracks, some spending as much as three weeks in the cars before they could leave.[167] The Red Cross estimated that over 17,000 Poinsett County residents had been driven from their homes by the 4th of February.[168]

A flood diary, found among the pages of an old business ledger in Paragould in early 2000, documents the activity over

---

[166] *Marked Tree Tribune*, February 4, 1937, 1.
[167] Prestidge, interview field notes.
[168] *Marked Tree Tribune*, February 4, 1937, 1.

a two-day period along the St. Francis River in Greene, Craighead, and Poinsett Counties. The keeper of the diary, C.W. Stedman of Paragould, had been recording weather data on a daily basis in the ledger all along, but in late December his recordings took on a desperate tone. When the water began topping the riverbanks and spilling over the land, Jonesboro radio station KBTM started a round-the-clock broadcast of flood information to direct help where it was needed. Stedman recorded many of the requests in his ledger, missing some because he writes that they were coming in too quickly to keep up with. They provide a fascinating, yet terrifying chronicle of the events as they unfolded.

According to the ledger beginning at 11:00 a.m. on January 22nd, KTBM reported that residents of Black Oak, Caraway, Monette, Lake City, Leachville, and Trumann were calling for boats and outside assistance, and that a woman was about to give birth while stranded on a rooftop at Lake City and a boat was needed immediately to rescue her. Rescuers reported that the woman and children of the little community of Lester were praying so loudly for help that they could be heard in the approaching boats. At 2:45 p.m. the station reported that the individual who was getting the woman off of the rooftop at Lake City was to meet an ambulance at the east end of the bridge so she could be taken to Jonesboro to the hospital. By 3:00 p.m. it was reported that both Paragould and East Arkansas Lumber Companies were building rescue boats as fast as they could to use in the rescue effort. At 4:40 p.m. a message was received from the Buffalo Island area that if motor boats did not reach Monette and Black Oak before dark they would all drown, and a caller from Poinsett County reported that everyone in Lepanto, Caraway, and Rivervale were standing in waist deep water and needed help immediately. The reports continued for two days until the crest was reached. Then the reports turned to help for the homeless.[169]

After the great flood of 1927 the U. S. Army Corps of Engineers created a series of flood control features that they called "Project Flood." At the northern end of the Lower Mississippi Valley they constructed a floodway that begins at Bird's Point, Missouri and extends for 65 miles to New Madrid, Missouri where anything in the area returns to the Mississippi. The levee at that section, called a fuse-plug levee, was designed to be lower than the rest of the levees along the river and is supposed to naturally blow out in a large flood. If it were to fail, then the Corps would use dynamite to blow a hole in it. The levee was designed to lower the river to protect the then-vital interior port city of Cairo, Illinois.[170] On January 25, 1937, the Corps dynamited the levee at Bird's Point to bring the water level down, probably taking some of the pressure off of the rivers downstream as well, but the rains continued to fall.

On February 11, a tent city at the county poor farm in Harrisburg housed 3,250 people. The *Marked Tree Tribune* that week reported the birth of twin boys to boxcar refugees, Mr. and Mrs. Arthur Pace of rural Tyronza. The boys were named Ed and Bob, after Poinsett County Red Cross director Ed Spees and Tyronza mayor Bob Frazier.[171] Refugees arrived to the various shelters cold and wet, many suffering from colds and pneumonia, as well as a number of communicable diseases. Health department authorities at Memphis stated that the situation was the greatest health hazard since the 1918

---

[169] Charles.W. Stedman, "Flood Diary and Business Ledger, 1936-1938", Greene County, Arkansas GenWeb. Accessed July 11, 2011 at 11:24 a.m. <http://www.argenweb.net/greene/GREENECOARLINKS/1937flooddiary.htm>

[170] John M. Barry, *Rising Tide: The Great Mississippi River Flood of 1927 and How It Changed America*, (New York: Touchstone Books, 1997), 423.

[171] An obituary for little Bob Pace was found in the *Marked Tree Tribune* less than a month later.

influenza outbreak.[172] In order to contain the infected, Red Cross officials met Arkansas refugees at the Harahan Bridge and escorted them to the fairgrounds where a camp had been set up and vaccinations were being given. Many though, were afraid of the situation in the camp and fearful of losing contact with their families as men and women were separated in barracks-like quarters. Consequently, they refused to follow Red Cross officials to the camps. They found shelter in abandoned homes and warehouses, or simply huddled together in alleys. Memphis officials' feared as many as 20,000 unvaccinated refugees were in the city and ordered the police department to round them up and take them to the fairgrounds. An outbreak of meningitis occurred in a refugee camp in Jonesboro. The patient, a young child, died within 48 hours and everyone who had contact with the family was ordered into isolation together. Thirty-six cases eventually were reported with 31 of them children. All five infected adults died of the disease and several of the children, but quick action by the staff at the camp averted what could have been an even worse disaster.[173]

Animals were another problem that flood-ravaged communities had to deal with. Delta plantations were still operating primarily with mules and livestock camps were set up to handle the influx of animals. Teddy Prestige recalled that his family's mules were moved to Jonesboro to be housed until the water went down and life could get back to normal. He remembers traveling to Jonesboro as a young boy to retrieve the mules and herd them back to Tyronza. The mule barn was located just east of the campus of what was then Arkansas State College and he remembers driving the mules down Aggie Road and then on to Highway 1, the current Caraway Road which then ran through the middle of the

---

[172] Patrick O'Daniel, *Memphis and the Super flood of 1937: High Water Blues,* (Charleston: The History Press, 2010), 58.
[173] American Red Cross, *The Ohio-Mississippi Valley Flood...*, 129.

campus, the mules scattering across the quad as they progressed on their way back toward home.[174]

With the flood over and things settling back down to normal, baseball returned to entertain the locals. By 1938, the Tyronza Independents were so well known for their expert level of play that they converted to an all-star format with players joining the team from as far away as Jonesboro. This new team included Arkansas State College's beloved young football coach, Leslie "Dukie" Speck. Desiring a regional identity for the team, the Independents nickname was dropped in favor of something more colorful. The team opened the 1938 season as the Poinsett Swamp Angels, and while they routinely routed opponents from much larger communities the Swamp Angels moniker was not long lived. After soundly defeating an all-star squad from Memphis, the losers taunted the Swamp Angels players saying their nickname made them sound like a malaria epidemic. Their winning streak intact but their pride injured, they came home and immediately decided to change their name. A vote among the players resulted in a switch to a more dignified, albeit less interesting sounding nickname and the Tyronza-Marked Tree Tigers were born. McDaniel, a major player in Democrat Party politics in the state, talked all of the Democrat candidates for local and county office that year into helping with the purchase of some snappy new matching blue and white uniforms to complete the transformation.[175]

The old pioneers in the planter-merchant class were beginning to fade away, death bringing a new generation to the forefront. The non-planter merchants like Jake Spiel passed on. He was replaced by his sons, Louis and Lester. Spiel was a

---

[174] Teddy Prestidge, Field Notes, Personal Interview with the author, Feb 25, 2008.

[175] In Poinsett County, like much of Arkansas, the majority of the candidates were Democrats and the Democrat Party primary usually decided the local elections.

Russian-born Jew and he was one of many such immigrants to make their home and their fortune in one of the small Delta farm towns. His business operated out of a section of Main Street called the Grossman Block which had been constructed by New York born Frank Grossman and his wife Sadie, who operated a dry goods store in the store front on the north end.[176] Another Jewish merchant, Philip Evensky, operated a store in the same building as Spiel and was one of several members of his immediate family to settle in the area, his brother Arthur owning a dry goods store in nearby Parkin. New immigrants made their way to the region from faraway places like China, Syria, Lebanon, and Italy. Among them was Joe Hong. Born in Canton, China he immigrated to the United States and opened a grocery on Main Street next door to City Drug Store. He served primarily the African-American sharecroppers and tenant farmers

On May 8, 1938 banker, merchant, planter, and early settler, John A. Emrich died. His oldest surviving son, John H. Emrich, took over the day-to-day operations of the business. The *Marked Tree Tribune* reported that the "colored people" of the community had asked to dig the elder Emrich's grave and hundreds of them had filed past his coffin at the cemetery, ending the service with an impromptu and stirring rendition of the spiritual, *Swing Low, Sweet Chariot*. Two years later, Lewis Wood, one half of the company of Wood and Warren Dry Goods, the duo who had originally purchased the old Ritter and Emrich store, also died.

The decade of the thirties had brought much in the way of disruption to Tyronza, but even that failed to slow the growth in the area. The 1940 Federal Census revealed that Poinsett County had recorded the largest gain in population in the

---

[176] Frank Grossman's brother, Jack operated a dry goods store in the neighboring town of Joiner in Mississippi County. In the 1930 census, he was the only non-Arab merchant in the town, the rest being natives of either Syria or Lebanon.

state with almost a twenty-seven percent increase. As the town emerged from two floods, a major drought, depressed farm prices, a radical labor union, and a socialist uprising, it seemed to be on the move with no end in sight. But a major disruption was about to occur. A good part of the world was already embroiled in another crisis that would soon pull the United States into the fray and start a revolution in the way business was done in the Delta.

Chapter 7
World War II and the Delta

Wealth has been taken out of this land in both timber and cotton but it has been completely taken out and away. There are few, if any, big houses and no evidence of planter grandeur beside the tenant poverty.

> Jonathan Daniels
> *A Southerner Discovers the South* (1939)

The Great Depression came to a close in the minds of the American people with the bombing of Pearl Harbor on December 7, 1941. With the United States entry into World War II, life in the Delta changed significantly. Thousands of young men and women left the rural areas bound for the military or jobs within the defense industry. Local planters hounded draft boards to exempt their best workers, but labor shortages resulted in these people demanding more than the planters believed they were worth. It was not unusual for a tenant to make a demand for something from the planter only to receive a draft notice for his trouble.[177] Wives and children of G.I.s who remained behind on the farm or in the small Delta towns received dependent checks from the government for living expenses. While they had willingly picked cotton for the low wages paid in the past, their new source of income left them not as needy of the extra cash earned from long, hot days in the fields chopping or picking cotton. To add to the planter's problems the once steady supply of temporary labor that had come down out of the hills were no longer available

---

[177] Pete Daniel, *Lost Revolutions: The South in the 1950's*, (Chapel Hill: University of North Carolina Press, 2000), 10.

either, pulled away from the old routines by the same jobs that attracted sharecroppers. Their absence created a labor shortage that could not be filled easily at the wages the planters wanted to pay.

Delta landowners had resisted mechanization for several years since so much of cotton farming still required extensive manual labor. While it was possible to plow and cultivate the plants with a tractor, eliminating the need for plowing with mules and hand chopping, there was still no reliable way to mechanically pick the cotton. This part of the process still required many hours of backbreaking labor. A mechanical cotton picker was finally developed in 1942 that would allow planters to fully mechanize the process. The labor shortage, combined with the extra money they had picked up from the federal government in the plow-up campaigns, provided the incentive many planters needed to take that final step. For numerous planters though, there was still a need for labor and they were able to subsidize their needs with an unlikely source, Axis prisoners of war.

Allied gains in the war, especially in Europe and North Africa, resulted in a tremendous influx of Axis prisoners of war into the continental United States. Over four hundred thousand German and Italian POWs were sent to camps in this country and nearly two-thirds of them spent time in the south. Here they worked in everything from local factories to saw mills to civic projects, taking the positions left behind by American workers who were supporting the war effort either in the trenches or the factories. The majority though, entered the agricultural fields picking everything from peanuts to cotton. The largest single group of POW labor toiled in the cotton fields of Arkansas, Mississippi, and Louisiana.[178]

---

[178] Jason Morgan Ward, ""Nazi's Hoe Cotton": Planters, POWs, and the Future of Farm Labor in the Deep South," *Agricultural History*, 81:4 (Fall, 2007), 473.

The state of Arkansas received approximately 23,000 enemy troops; most were members of Germany's famed Afrika Korps, headed by the notorious Field Marshal Erwin Rommel. During the first two years of the war, the government had failed to prepare for the eventual possibility of enemy prisoners on the home front, but the mass surrender of Axis troops in the North African theater resulted in a scramble for facilities. Military installations and even some federal civilian facilities were pressed into service in a short time. Three camps were established in Arkansas: Camp Robinson, Camp Chaffee, and Camp Dermott. The largest of the three was Camp Robinson which was designed to hold over 5,000 POWs in two separate areas, but the need for space was great and thirty-one branch camps were established throughout the state to house additional men. Most of these were in the Delta, including two in Poinsett County.

In the fall of 1943 the War Department, the War Food Administration, and the War Manpower Commission (WMC) worked out a suitable arrangement for making POW labor available to local employers. The WMC determined that if a need for labor existed and if there was an insufficient local labor force to fill those jobs, then POWs could be used. The employer, or planter as was the case in the Delta, entered into a contract in which they promised to pay the prevailing local wage and to care for the prisoners in a specified manner. The Geneva Convention required each POW be allowed to keep eighty cents of his daily wage, while the rest was paid to the United States Treasury to pay for his upkeep.[179] In Poinsett County, a second generation of planter-businessmen had taken over the reins of the empires created by their fathers. Louis V. Ritter, Sr. and his brother Harry[180] had taken over the

---

[179] Merrill Pritchett and William L. Shea, "The Afrika Korps in Arkansas, 1943-1946," *The Arkansas Historical Quarterly*, 37:1 (Spring, 1978), 13.
[180] Harry married Margaret Emrich, oldest daughter of John A. and Rose Emrich. While the couple made their home in neighboring Marked Tree

business created by their father after the elder man's death in 1921. Louis organized a group of local planters called the Delta Association which managed to attract a POW camp to neighboring Marked Tree.[181] The camp, which housed three hundred fifty prisoners, was built on land owned by Chapman and Dewey, with lumber furnished by the Delta Association. John H. Emrich, the son of Tyronza's first banker and now owner and operator of the family business, employed many German prisoners in his gin in Tyronza. They would leave the gin every day at noon under guard and cross the street to the Midway Café for lunch, eating with the locals.[182]

In 1942, the United States entered into a joint project with the Mexican government to allow thousands of Mexican nationals to cross the border to work as seasonal labor in the agricultural industry. Known as the Bracero Program, landowners were required to pick up laborers at border stations, pay $25 per person, and transport them back to their farms where they provided a paycheck, food, and shelter. Even with this additional labor, the need for workers was overwhelming. Prices for cotton pickers rose from one dollar

---

they maintained a connection to Tyronza through Margaret's work in the family business.

[181] *Marked Tree Tribune*, May 11, 1944, p.1. Ritter served as a director of the group along with Tyronza residents Herrick Norcross and J.H. Prestidge, as well as Lepanto businessmen D.F. Portis and J.G. Stuckey, and Trumann's Dr. G.O. Campbell.

[182] It is fascinating to think about the social dynamics of having German prisoners of war integrated into the everyday world of a place like Tyronza. The Midway Café, where the POWs ate their lunch every workday with the townspeople, sat squarely in the middle of the Grossman block which had been built by Jewish businessman Frank Grossman. Three other Jewish families operated businesses in the same building. Bette Evensky Greene, a resident of Parkin in Cross County and the niece of Tyronza businessman Philip Evensky, chronicles such issues in her 1973 book, *Summer of My German Soldier*, a fictional account which deals with these issues as she experienced them during the war. It is also notable to realize that while German POWs could eat in the Midway, African American sharecroppers, among them soldiers fighting for the Allied cause, could not.

per one hundred pounds of cotton in 1941 to three dollars per hundred in 1944.[183] This additional source of labor allowed the tenant farming system to remain viable until people began returning home after the war.

With the war came a new burst of energy by Tyronza's people. The town again answered the call to support the troops with the local women spending two days a week doing Red Cross work at the Methodist Church. The men organized a war bond drive with a goal of $50,000. Tyronza was the only town in Arkansas to not only reach its goal but surpass it, selling over $55,000 in bonds. A second drive was organized by Tyronza school children. They sold enough bonds to purchase a jeep for the military.[184]

On September 7, 1944, the *Marked Tree Tribune* reported that fifteen Poinsett County landowners had watched a demonstration of a new mechanical cotton picker. Although only thirty-five demonstration units were in operation at the time, the machine was planned for mass production and would soon be easily available. International Harvester's picker would do the work of 50 humans and would effectively drop the production price per bale from just over $39 to $5.[185] The demonstration signaled a great change in agriculture in the not-so-distant future. It would also indicate a great change in the future of Tyronza, a town whose very survival depended on farming.

Changes in agriculture also resulted from other innovations. New fertilizers were increasing yields while insecticides were taking their toll on boll weevils and other pests. The *Marked Tree Tribune* reported on April 12, 1945, that fifty-three hundred Poinsett County homes were going to be sprayed with the new miracle insecticide called DDT which would rid

---

[183] John Solomon Otto, *The Final Frontier, 1880-1930: Settling the Southern Bottomlands.* (Westport, CT: Greenwood Press, 1999),111.
[184] "Tyronza reaches goal", *Marked Tree Tribune*, December 28, 1944, 1.
[185] Otto, *The Final Frontier,* 111.

the Delta of the mosquito, taking malaria with it for good. County Health Department crews entered rural homes and sprayed everything including bedding and kitchens.[186] It would be years before environmentalist Rachel Carson would publish her explosive book, *Silent Spring*, and bring awareness of the health damage that had been inflicted on innocent people and animals. In the meantime, the spraying would continue.

The end of the war brought new changes to the people of the Delta. Many of its most promising young people, both rich and poor, black and white, realized that times were changing and if they returned to their old lives in northeast Arkansas, the world might leave them behind. They fled to the universities for an education promised by the G.I. Bill, or to union jobs on Ford, Chrysler, and General Motors assembly lines in Detroit, Chicago, and St. Louis. They left for cities and better lives all over the country. For those who remained the next few years would bring an end to a way of life that was all they had ever known.

---

[186] Pete Daniel, *Toxic Drift: Pesticides and Health in the Post-World War II South*, (Baton Rouge: Louisiana State University Press, 2005), 65.

Logging railroad "dummy line" near Parkin in Cross County. The name dummy line comes from the fact that this is a false railroad, or temporary. Note this one has the rails laid across logs rather than ties. William Beasley's Tyronza Lumber and Cooperage Company operated a line similar to this one from Tyronza to Marlin's Swamp. It was demolished before 1907. Photo courtesy Parkin Archeological State Park.

A cotton field in cultivation in the cutover land, among the stumps and fallen trees. This was a common sight in the early years around Tyronza. Photo courtesy Parkin Archeological State Park.

The 1913 flood at Tyronza forced many residents to move to the high ground that the railroad provided. In the background is the Dr. E.C. McDaniel home that still stands on Frisco Street. To the right is the remains of Ann Stalker's mound where her home sat until it was demolished for a newer structure. Photo courtesy Southern Tenant Farmers Museum.

Oliver Davis, one of the Tyronza's early settlers and businessmen. Photo courtesy Southern Tenant Farmers Museum.

Corner of Main and Frisco Streets about 1916. To the right is John Emrich's Bank of Tyronza and the large building to the left held the firm of Ritter & Emrich, General Merchandise. They sold out shortly after this photo was taken to Wood & Warren Dry Goods. The street was still dirt at this time, but the sidewalks in front of the businesses are concrete. They turn to wood as they round the edge of the bank building. Photo courtesy Southern Tenant Farmers Museum.

A 1903 photo of the students at the Tyronza Public School shows 36 pupils and a dog. This building sat across the street from the current school on the site of the Tyronza Church of Christ. It was replaced by a larger wooden structure that sat near the intersection of Church and Beasley Streets. Photo courtesy Southern Tenant Farmers Museum.

Tyronza High School. This modern, architect designed building was erected in 1916 and illustrates the rapid growth of the school aged population in the town. Photo courtesy Southern Tenant Farmers Museum.

The Poinsett Swamp Angels in 1938. Shortly after this photo was taken the team rechristened themselves the Tyronza-Marked Tree Tigers. Dr. L.H. McDaniel, the team's manager and coach, is pictured on the front row in the center. The three men on the back row are local businessmen who provided financial backing for the team. Photo courtesy Southern Tenant Farmers Museum.

Mac Howard's Café was located next door to the Tyronza Supply building. Howard was an interesting character who served for a time as the city marshal. It was known to be a wild place and was supposedly the impetus for Tyronza's prohibition on alcohol which was instituted during World War II at a time when the female population well outnumbered the males. Photo courtesy Southern Tenant Farmers Museum.

The Midway Café probably in the late 1940's. During World War II it was not uncommon to see a line of German prisoners of war from the Marked Tree Branch Camp, marched across the street each day at noon from the Tyronza Gin to eat their lunch among the locals. It is still in business today in its original location in the Grossman Block on Main Street. Photo courtesy Southern Tenant Farmers Museum.

The Tyronza General Supply in the 1940's. The building was originally constructed by Van Young and Mac Howard. They lost the business and John A. Emrich moved his mercantile into the structure and his children operated it until the 1970's. It has been purchased by the Upper Room Apostolic Church and they are converting it to an education building. Photo courtesy Southern Tenant Farmers Museum.

Braceros in the 1950's in Tyronza. The high school offered Spanish language classes in the evenings for local residents so they could more easily converse with the farm workers. Photo courtesy Southern Tenant Farmers Museum.

General William Westmoreland visits Tyronza as a guest of Dr. L.H. McDaniel in the 1950's The general was the uncle of McDaniel's son-in-law, Thomas Woodruff. Dr. McDaniel and R.D. Gill stand to the right of the general. Photo courtesy Southern Tenant Farmers Museum.

Main Street in Tyronza was still a busy place in the 1950's. Both the Western Auto store on the right and the block containing City Drug Store on the left have since burned. A Greyhound bus can be seen on the right. A second bus terminal was housed in Joe Hong's store across the street. Photo courtesy Southern Tenant Farmers Museum.

The Tyro Theatre in the mid 1950's was a busy place. It had first run movies every night and matinee's on Saturday. It was located between the old Odd Fellows Hall and the Tyronza Supply in the location which now holds the Upper Room Apostolic Church. Photo courtesy Southern Tenant Farmers Museum.

Joe Hong stands in front of his store about 1965 and shortly before he closed his doors for good. He moved to Tyronza from Canton, China in the mid 1930's to open a grocery serving primarily the African American and sharecropper community. He left to open a grocery in Memphis which he operated until his death in 1976. Photo courtesy Southern Tenant Farmers Museum.

Chapter 8
Times of Change

It happened in the middle 1960s, at the end of an era — an era not fading into antiquity so much as it was being gnawed away. The big mechanical pickers, like giant, chewing pests, had arrived in the red-dirt fields of the foothills, tearing through the fields, leaving the cotton dirty and half picked, ripped into scrap. Pickers of flesh and blood, seasonal workers who picked to make a little extra cash, were obsolete. The future ran on diesel, and it didn't even pick clean.
Rick Bragg
The Most They Ever Had
(2009)

The 1950s were the time of greatest change in Tyronza and the surrounding area. The election of 1952 brought Dwight D. Eisenhower to the White House, and with his presidency Arkansas farmers would never be the same. Again it would be the Secretary of Agriculture who would have the most impact on the lives and economy of Tyronza residents and indeed of rural residents all over America. Eisenhower selected for the position an Idaho farmer and university extension agent named Ezra Taft Benson. Benson was a devout Mormon, a member of the select Quorum of Twelve Apostles, and later served as President of the LDS Church. He was strongly supportive of mechanization and scientific agriculture. America was in the midst of the Cold War and national strength was the goal of everyone in the administration. Benson believed that farmers should be weaned off of the federal subsidy programs that had started during the New Deal, asserting that the market would stabilize everything. In order to accomplish this market-driven agriculture, the least efficient farmers had to go. He encouraged mechanization, and the increased use of fertilizers and pesticides. He wanted farmers to "get big or get out."[187]

With the increases in chemical usage came increases in yield. American farmers, including those in Poinsett County, became ruthlessly efficient. The increased harvests resulted in a surplus which brought about a drop in price. Benson responded by instituting a Soil Bank under Title I of the Agricultural Act of 1956 which allowed farm owners to retire land from production under two separate programs. The Acreage Reserve Program (ARP) allowed them to enter into one-year contracts during the years 1956 through 1959; and the Conservation Reserve Program (CRP) allowed them to sign extended contracts of three, five, and ten years. For the first time in history, farm land was worth more idle than in production. As in the past, planters controlled the local boards and directed wealth in their direction. Their remaining tenants were either displaced or hired as day laborers, and that land went into the Soil Banks.[188] The reduction in productive land led to a ripple effect across the South. The economy slowed in the farm towns as less cotton grown meant less ginning, less equipment to be sold, and less fertilizer to be spread.[189]

The ARP and CRP also meant fewer people, for the demand for tenants to work the land also dropped dramatically and Tyronza felt the changes. In 1956, the First Baptist Church owned three buses that were used to haul farm families from the rural areas into the town for Sunday school and church services. The next year they sold them all for there were so few

---

[187] Pete Daniel, *Toxic Drift: Pesticides and Health in the Post-World War II South,* (Baton Rouge: Louisiana State University Press, 2005),, 1.
[188] Pete Daniel, *Lost Revolutions: The South in the 1950s*, (Chapel Hill: University of North Carolina Press, 2000), 56.
[189] Ibid, 57.

people left to bring in on Sunday for services that it was no longer feasible to keep them.

With few sharecroppers left in the area and most of the merchants closing their doors, many of the town's leading families pulled up stakes and moved to places with a brighter future.[190] The 1950s also saw the Arkansas Highway and Transportation Department construct a bypass around the town, abandoning the concrete highway that the townspeople had built in the 1920s. Cars full of shoppers now headed directly to Memphis without passing through Tyronza's business district. Many of Tyronza's merchants simply shuttered their now silent stores and moved their merchandise and their families to Memphis.

By the time the 1960s rolled around, commerce in Tyronza was in serious decline. Businessmen continued to leave town, membership in civic groups slacked off, and the community began to die. The revered town doctor, L.H. McDaniel, known throughout the community and the country for his attempts to breathe new life in both people and places, had attempted to bolster the town by bringing people and ideas to the populace throughout the fifties and early sixties. Tyronza residents were just as likely to see the governor of the state, the commanding General of the Army, or a professional baseball player at the store as they were to see an old friend. McDaniel brought an assortment of dignitaries to Tyronza to speak at Rotary Club meetings, to address the school children, or to help boost the economy with first one scheme then another.

A devout Christian and leader in the medical community, McDaniel started a biennial conference in 1952 of medical and dental practitioners called the Festival of Faith in Tyronza. The event was designed to encourage not only the health care profession, but government and civic leaders, and

---

[190] John Wayne Austin, Field Notes, Personal Interview with the author, Tyronza, AR, September 27, 2008.; and, Teddy Prestidge, Field Notes, Personal Interview with the author, Feb 25, 2008.

townspeople as a whole to embrace their neighbor's concern as their own and work together. Two local African American men, George Fischer and Gilbert Duncan, were hired by McDaniel to barbeque huge amounts of meat over an open pit for the two-day event. Both men were well known in the community for their cooking and were often hired by the white planters to accompany them on their large hunts and do the cooking.[191] Local women, like Mrs. Hiram Norcross, assisted by hosting teas for the wives of visitors. The Festival of Faith was held in a circus tent on the grounds of the high school and brought thousands to the town. The last event in 1962 brought an estimated 5,000 people to the little community and included such personages as Dr. Norman Vincent Peale and comedian Danny Thomas. The governors of seven Southern states attended the festival that year as well. On April 7, 1965, while planning the next festival, Dr. McDaniel died in a Memphis hospital of a heart attack. The town seemed to die with him.[192]

The year 1960 would mark the first time in the history of Tyronza that its population declined, falling from 656 in 1950, to 601. In 1965 the Frisco Railroad stopped passenger service along the Kansas City to Memphis line and tore down the depot, the place that had been the center of the community since it was built in the 1880s. Two years later Joe Hong, the immigrant from China who had arrived in 1937 to open a store and restaurant, closed his doors for good in Tyronza. He stayed on ten years longer than the rest and he lamented years later that he should have left sooner, but just could not bring himself to pull up stakes and move on.

---

[191] Prestidge, Field Notes. Teddy Prestidge recalled that when George Fischer died in 1953, the pallbearers at his funeral were the white planters from the community, but that when Gilbert died a few years later, no whites attended his funeral. Asked why, he responded "That integration mess had come about by then."

[192] Calvin Hill McDaniel, Field Notes, interview with the author, Tyronza, AR, October 4, 2008; Austin, Field Notes,; and Prestidge, Field Notes.

By 1970 the town could claim only 510 residents, the lowest population since the incorporation of the town in 1926, and even lower than the estimated population in 1920. An exodus away from Southern cities began in the late 1960s with the changes brought about by the Civil Rights movement. White flight was rampant with people looking for places to settle down. Tyronza, with its location on a major highway halfway between Memphis and the education and commercial center of Jonesboro, was a natural location for new settlement. Local landowner and lifelong resident, George Beley, whose father had come to Tyronza in the 1920s to buy cotton and fell in love with one of the East girls and stayed on to run his business in town, converted a portion of the family farm (between downtown Tyronza and the school), into a subdivision. Filling it with Farmers Home Administration and Veterans Administration loan-approved homes, he attracted young families to the community. The influx of new students encouraged the members of the local school board who voted to replace the aging school with a new modern building. Tyronza was on the move again and by 1980 the population was at an all-time high of 777 residents.

Even though the population continued to increase with each successive decade, rather than becoming a thriving business community again, the town became a bedroom community. Businesses continued to close their doors as residents picked up the items they needed on their way home from work in the larger cities. In 1976, the Emrich family's Tyronza General Supply which had operated first as a general merchandise store during the timber years then converted to a plantation commissary during the sharecropping times, closed its doors for good. In 1986, Tyronza lost its high school when the district voted to merge with neighboring Lepanto creating the East Poinsett County School District, and the older students were bused there. With the loss of the high school came a loss of local identity as the Tyronza Chiefs failed to take the football field in the fall of 1986 for the first time since they fielded that first six-man team fifty years earlier.

The 1990s brought more people to live in the town but fewer to shop there. Businesses continued to close as more and more people traveled to Jonesboro or Memphis to spend their money and leisure time. The 2000 census showed Tyronza at an all-time high of 918 residents. The town appeared to be bucking the trends that plagued so many other Delta communities although the downtown was dying quickly. The children of the young families that had made Tyronza home in the 70s and 80s followed the rest of their peers to the city and the population began to age. About that time, a local resident named John Wayne Austin convinced some of the other residents of the town that they needed to do something to salvage what they had. He recognized the national significance of the Southern Tenant Farmers Union and the small group approached Arkansas State University about saving the building that had housed H.L. Mitchell's dry cleaning establishment and Clay East's gas station and had served as the unofficial offices of the union during its first year of existence, and creating a museum. In 2001 they approached Dr. Ruth Hawkins of the university's Arkansas Heritage Sites office to assist them in finding the needed funding to save the structures. The university decided to preserve the structure as the home of the Southern Tenant Farmers Museum and launched both a restoration and a research project. Unanticipated restoration expenses resulted in the building, with most of the exhibits already created and installed, sitting idle for almost a year while waiting for additional grant funding to complete it. Further complications arose when the funding for daily operations that the city had worked to acquire through their local elected state representatives did not materialize. Hawkins and the university's Heritage Studies PhD program students soldiered on and in October 2006 the museum opened with a large opening ceremony.

There was hope that the presence of the museum would heal old wounds and bring new life to the town by encouraging the local residents to invest in new businesses and recreating the community that had been diminished by the loss of the school.[193]

In 2008, East Poinsett County school officials began looking at the future of the aging facilities at both Lepanto and Tyronza. Both structures are in need of repair and the money is not there to complete them. Plans were in the works to close the school at Tyronza and build a new elementary building at Lepanto consolidating all administrative functions on one campus. Tyronza would be left without its own school for the first time in over one hundred years. Townspeople resigned themselves to believe the eventual closing inevitable and that there is nothing they can do to stop it.

Today the town is only a shell of its former self. The city government continues to function, it does so on a limited budget that barely covers its needs. The downtown finally was placed on the National Register of Historic Places in 2010, a first step in the process toward possibly revitalizing the area, but only weeks after the nomination was final, a fire wiped out an entire block of the business district across from the City Hall. The structures that once housed Joe Hong's Grocery, Dr. Boone's dental office, Dr. McDaniel's medical practice, and the City Drug Store are gone. One of the only surviving businesses in the town, Wilson Funeral Home, which was housed in the remains of Joe Hong's old store was destroyed as well.

---

[193] Hawkins had good reason to think as she did. The university had restored a house belonging to Paul and Mary Pfeiffer of Piggott a few years earlier, and had created a house museum to honor both them and their well known son-in-law Ernest Hemingway. The creation of the Hemingway-Pfeiffer Home and Educational Center had spurred a good deal of interest from the general public and the town had responded by opening new businesses to cater to the increased traffic flow. Eighteen new tourism related businesses opened in the first two years.

Currently the business district consists of an auto parts store, the post office, a branch of the First Delta Bank headquartered in Marked Tree, a convenience store, a café, the funeral home, and the museum. The parts store is family-owned and may not survive much longer. The post office faces automation like so many others in the country as the United States Postal Service looks for ways to cut costs and remain competitive, but apparently will survive the round of closings projected by the postal service to take place in 2012. The convenience store changes managers every year, leased by first one outside interest then another. The funeral home has been rebuilt after the fire on a lot next to its former location in a brick building that blends better with the rest of the downtown, but even that business is slow.

The town is still pretty. The city retained the services of Marion Burke to sweep the streets with a push broom to keep them clean. Five mornings a week, winter or summer, you could find him there. The locals would slow down and drive around him as to not disturb his work, but shortly after the fire the mayor relieved him of the job. She believed he was no longer healthy enough to continue. For a while he would wander along the streets with nothing to do, or just sit and watch traffic for hours on end, but recently purchased an electric mobility chair and now zips all over town in it.

Two city employees mow all city-owned property as well as the ditches and right of ways along the streets to keep them maintained and attractive. City residents do their part by keeping their lawns and homes in tiptop condition. A move back toward the urban core began a few years ago and many blighted downtown areas have been brought back to life, with new housing available for young professionals and their families, with Memphis working hard to attract young professionals back to its core. Inner-city schools are being targeted for improvement and they are making great strides every day, while rural schools are suffering. In 2011, the

Memphis Public Schools, which had suffered for years while young families fled to the rural areas, disbanded and requested to be consolidated into the better funded Shelby County School District, in the hope that the influx of capital will bring about much needed improvements to the city's schools. To the north, Jonesboro has been in the midst of a population boom fueled by both the university and continued growth in the industrial sector. Fuel prices and a concern for the environment are beginning to reverse the desire for everyone to own a car and drive it as much as they possibly can. Towns like Tyronza – without a commercial core, possibly without a school, and without an identity – are being abandoned to those who cannot escape and the blight that was once the reason for moving to the rural area, is now a rural problem. The 2010 census revealed a rapidly decreasing population with only 762 residents still calling Tyronza home.

Better times may be on the horizon though. The old Tyronza General Supply building was in a state of decay that seemed almost irreversible. The roof had collapsed, the windows were broken, and the front awning has begun to fall. The land around the building which once housed a restaurant and gas station were piled up with junked cars and trucks. The building was purchased by the Upper Room Apostolic Church who at first wanted to demolish the building but later determined that too much history had gone on there to tear it down. They are in the process of refurbishing the old building for use as an educational wing. Across the street, a local couple Keith and Jill Forrester who are among the Delta's new breed of entrepreneurs, have started work on the old Tyronza Grocery building to use as a restaurant and produce market. A new senior citizens/community center, constructed with USDA funds, opened between City Hall and the Southern Tenant Farmers Museum. While its future as a senior citizen center is in flux, the building stands as a testament to future commitment to growth by the townspeople.

The place that is now Tyronza has experienced a great deal of change since its inception in 1884. The landscape has been altered to such an extent that Ann Stalker would not recognize it. The mounds that survived from the town's earliest residents have been leveled. The cabins and shacks that lined the roads radiating from the town and housed three generations of timber men and sharecroppers have been pushed down and burned to make room for more cotton.[194] The railroad that opened the town and the region up to the rest of the world failed to stop again in the mid 1960s and the depot – once the heart of Tyronza – was torn down. The Greyhound and Trailways bus lines no longer stop to pick up or drop off passengers. The streets that once held one thousand people on a Saturday night during the Great Depression are often empty. Tyronza may one day be like the earlier community that existed on this site, forgotten.

Rural America is dying or at least being pushed aside, reorganized into regional population centers. In the year 2000 nearby Jonesboro reached a population milestone of 50,000 residents officially achieving metropolitan status. All of the people of Craighead and Poinsett Counties, including Tyronza, are now lumped into the area called the Jonesboro Metropolitan Statistical Area. While the additions are good news for Jonesboro as it fights for tax dollars to pay for needed improvements, where does it leave Tyronza?

Can the town that during the first World War raised seventeen thousand dollars and sent dozens of sweaters to the soldiers, while nursing their own during the Spanish Flu pandemic, save itself? Can the town that survived the 1927 flood, followed by a two-year drought, and then a Stock Market crash survive? Can the town that survived a planter-sharecropper standoff and the 1937 flood, while supporting a refugee population of its own size, in the middle of the Great Depression, create a new economy? Can the town that was the

---

[194] Daniel, *Lost Revolutions*, 7.

only one in the state to surpass its war bond quota in World War II and successfully host a nationally renowned medical convention in a circus tent come back? Will Tyronza survive.

Chapter Nine
The Aftermath

I woke up this morning thinking this town might as well be standing on the absolute floor of hell for all the truth this is in it, and the fault is mine as much as anyone's. I was thinking about the things that had happened here just in my lifetime—the droughts and the influenza and the Depression and three terrible wars. It seems to me now we never looked up from the trouble we had just getting by to put the obvious question, that is to ask what it was the Lord was trying to make us understand.

Marilynne Robinson
Gilead (2004)

A person's feelings about a place change over time but in different ways for different people. With the thirtieth anniversary of my high school reunion coming up next year I have noticed a good deal of reminiscing among my old high school friends from my hometown in Missouri. For those who left shortly after high school for college, a job, or the military, there is much talk of old times and how wonderful the town was to grow up in. Among those who remain there is discussion of shared lives, children growing up together, and familiar feelings about what a nice place it still is. I was one of the ones who stayed for a while then moved on. Divorced at twenty-seven, I left the old town behind along with some bad memories and headed off to make a new life in the historic Mississippi River town of Hannibal, Missouri. While I was gone, the old town experienced a renaissance of sorts with a population and building boom that left Hannibal seeming old and worn out. After a couple of years I headed home to what looked like a better life, but the adage that says, "You can't go home again" held true. Things had not really changed all that much except in a physical way.

Eugene Walter's theory that says we place a greater emphasis on the physical than the logical proved true in my case. Feelings about a place can shift over time, but it requires a complete paradigm change for it to happen. Tyronza for the first few decades of its existence experienced those types of change, from a wilderness where Ann Stalker and her family could just disappear, to Billy Beasley's timber empire, then on to a small farm town, and eventually to a plantation town. The final change occurred when the plantation changed to a corporation and many of the people ceased to have a place in the community. They included the most marginalized, the sharecroppers and tenant farmers, followed by the day laborers who stayed around earning extra money in the fall during picking time until the mechanical pickers replaced them too. These people were followed by the merchants, first the immigrants like the Grossmans, the Spiels, and the Evenskys, followed a few years later by Joe Hong and his family. Then the sons and the daughters of the planters and merchants moved on, leaving one or two among them to run the operation and send the checks for their portion of the proceeds to the rest in far-away cities like Los Angeles, Boston, and Atlanta.

Although the sharecroppers were gone they left behind remnants of their being in and around Tyronza and the hundreds of other towns just like it, the farmers who were left bulldozed and burned the physical structures of these people; the shacks, juke joints, schools, churches, and in many cases cemeteries, are now gone to make room for more cotton. The spaces of these people were destroyed as if that alone would erase them from the history of the place. They did a pretty effective job. A close look at the 1936 general highway map for Poinsett County shows thousands of homes and gathering places lining the roads surrounding places like Tyronza, a blackened-in square representing an individual house. Each one of those blackened squares held a family who lived, loved, and died on that land. You can look at a modern general highway map and see the results of mechanization. The map shows a stark place. Tyronza Township was once covered in squares and lines representing people and homes and roads they lived in and worked on. Today, the houses are gone along with many of the roads, replaced by acres of cultivated land. All in the name of progress.

There is a song by Joni Mitchell called "Big Yellow Taxi" in which she laments:

> *Don't it always seem to go*
> *That you don't know what you've got*
> *Till it's gone*
> *They paved paradise*
> *And put up a parking lot*[195]

It may be difficult to think of rows of sharecropper shacks as paradise but they were home for thousands who still think of the flat land around Tyronza, where their lives were anything but easy, as home.

Planter families will tell you that they loved their sharecroppers and tenants and that they were like family to them. That may be so, as long as they were necessary for the completion of the job which was to plant and chop and pick the cotton that paid the bills on the plantation, but once these people could be replaced with machines and chemicals they were cast aside along with any vestige of their existence. That being said, people like Teddy Prestidge, himself the son of a planter, laments the loss of that way of life and the community that went with it, in spite of the union and the problems it caused in the town, but he is one of the few because he is one of the only ones who can truly remember what it was like.

---

[195] Original lyrics by Joni Mitchell at <http://jonimitchell.com/music/song.cfm?id=208>

Those who remained in the town, whose work was not lost to the tractor and Round-Up, lived in nice homes with small lawns and little landscaping, in order to use as much tillable land as possible for crops. They make money but spend it elsewhere, primarily Memphis, but often Dallas or Atlanta. They have in many ways given up their identification as landed gentry and instead become agribusiness men. Their children moved away. The town was in many ways treated the same way as the sharecroppers. Businesses failed, churches closed, and community life flickered and in many cases died.

In the twenty years after World War II, eleven million rural Southerners left the farm.[196] These rural poor, the sharecroppers and tenant farmers, lacked the formal education and skills necessary to shift easily into urban life. They experienced the extreme alienation in their new homes known as anomie. While they suffered in their new homes, they spread a southern culture, both black and white, into new parts of the country bringing their food and music to a new crowd. The result for the country was culture change that rocked the nation.[197]

The Southern Tenant Farmers Union has been looked at by many scholars as the source of the downfall of Tyronza. It has been assumed that the actions of the townspeople and the planters acted like a cancer that ate away at the community, but in reality it was the change in the agricultural model. The planters who had fought government intrusion into their lives in the 1930s now were concerned only with who could get the

---

[196] Pete Daniel, *Lost Revolutions: The South in the 1950s,*. (Chapel Hill: University of North Carolina Press, 2000), 39.

[197] Wanda Rushing, *Memphis and the Paradox of Place: Globalization in the American South,* (Chapel Hill: University of North Carolina Press, 2009), 25. Barbeque and a new musical tradition entered the national identity after the war. The Delta Blues had found a home in places like Chicago as early as the 1920s but was joined by country, bluegrass, southern gospel, rock and roll, and rockabilly.

most, for business is business and that is the only way to survive.[198]

The rural Delta of today is greatly different from the place it was in 1934. The highways are empty of houses and generally the people you see are in the cab of a tractor or puncturing the giant white rolls of filled poly pipe with a tool that lets the water flow. The overuse of chemicals throughout the years has resulted in herbicide resistant strains of weeds like pigweed that require human choppers to come back into the fields to clear them. The past couple of years I have seen more and more of them, walking the rows in the oppressive summer heat, a straw hat and a long sleeved shirt their main protection against the sun, with a chopping hoe in their hands. Everything old is new again.

During my short stay in Tyronza my feelings about the place shifted from one extreme to the other. Most days I was excited about the possibilities of what lay in store for a town that took such good care of itself despite the lack of funds. I went out on a balmy, but overcast, March day to do a photo shoot on Main Street. I wanted to look at it through a new set of eyes, to take in the sights of the town in a different way. It left me exhilarated. One year to the day later I went back out to have another look and I remember coming back in feeling defeated and disheartened. The town was literally falling down before my eyes.

I do not want it to fail, but I understand that it must eventually. It may not be tomorrow, but someday soon unless it again reinvents itself to thrive once more, if only for a short time.

---

[198] Ibid, 10.

Appendix
Searching For Mrs. Stalker

I first learned of the existence of the woman I now know as Ann Stalker in 2006. I saw her name on a small granite marker in the little park generally known as the Church Park that sits midway down Main Street across the street from the Supply. When I launched my search for Tyronza's history a few months later, I came across her name again at the University of Arkansas archives in the records of the Tyronza Ginning Company. The older boxes contained several deeds of trust between John A. Emrich and other former residents who had either sold him land outright or lost it to pay off a crop lien.

Emrich had purchased land from Mrs. Martha Stalker that included the notation that the parcel was missing a two-acre lot that had been deeded to the Missionary Baptist Association for the building of a church. That lot corresponded with the location of the park and it fit with a story that Teddy Prestige had once told me about the park at one time being the site of a community church that had served the town until the late 1920s. It also corresponded with the location of Emrich's home which sat just to the south of the church lot. When I asked about her around town, the people who did know the name only knew it from the naming of the park. It seemed that she played a role in the formation of the town, but no one could provide any useful details.

I made a trip a short time later to the state archives in Little Rock to see if there was anything available on Tyronza's past. My search turned up short biographies on John A. Emrich and Dr. L.H. McDaniel and a reference to a place called Tyronza Station in an old journal of a man named Edward Palmer. The journal was a handwritten affair that had been microfilmed and turned out to be the travel journal of a Smithsonian Institute ethnologist who had travelled to Arkansas in the early 1880s to oversee a survey that the organization had ordered on the thousands of earthen mounds in the Ohio and Mississippi River Valleys and across the southeastern United States.[199] There was an entry for Tyronza Station, as the place was called at the time, that described the land forms and mentioned that Mrs. Martha Stalker had presented to the United States of America a fine water jar and two knives she had unearthed while plowing. This was intriguing to say the least. At this time, the town was no more than a railroad siding and she was already here, farming the land, seemingly alone. It appeared that she must be a widow as she was referred to as Mrs. Stalker. Were there children? How old was she? What happened to her husband? Most importantly, what happened to her?

For many years, I worked in the criminal justice field, so any type of mystery intrigued me. This woman was a mystery so I launched a search for her. As a long time genealogist I was very familiar with research using the United States Federal

---

[199] Credit for the construction of the mounds had long been given to the native peoples of the area by observers such as Thomas Jefferson who did work on mounds located on his property at Monticello in Virginia, but the federal government's relocation program hinged on the premise that the aboriginal peoples of North America were less than human and certainly not intelligent enough to design and build these structures. When the results of the survey indicated that the Native Americans were indeed responsible for the mounds, the government simply chose to ignore it. The survey report has been published and makes for fascinating reading. See Cyrus Thomas, *Report on the Mound Explorations of the Bureau of Ethnology*, (Washington, DC: Smithsonian Institution Press), 1985. Palmer's journal of his time in Arkansas was edited by Arkansas Archeological Survey archeologist Marvin Jeter. In addition to the wonderful information on the mounds and the people who once inhabited the state, there are amazing descriptions of Arkansas towns and stories of the people with whom he stayed during his travels. They make for great reading and illustrate the lives and customs of many of the people, like Mrs. Stalker, who otherwise would go unrecognized. See Marvin D. Jeter, ed., *Edward Palmer's Arkansaw Mounds*. (Fayetteville: University of Arkansas Press), 1990.

Census records. I began with the federal census for Poinsett County on the internet genealogy site *Ancestry.com* as that was the closest enumeration of Palmer's interaction with Stalker. I located a woman named M.A. Stocker in Little River Township in the index and pulled up the digital copy to have a look. M.A. Stocker was a widow, forty-two years old with four children in the home and a hired man named J.H. Rushing. Could this be Martha Stalker? Census takers were notoriously bad spellers and the census indicated that this M.A. Stocker could neither read nor write, so she would have been of little help as he tried to sound it out. If the family had lived here long it was doubtful that any of the children had ever attended school. The children ranged in age from a twenty-one-year-old son to a four-year-old daughter. If this little girl was the child of the husband then he had died within the past four years.

Armed with this bit of knowledge, I headed to the Poinsett County Courthouse in Harrisburg to see if I could locate a land record for anyone named Stocker or Stalker. I found a deed of trust dated April, 1876 between N.B. Martis and Duncan Stocker and Martha A. Stocker, his wife. The Stockers had purchased a quarter section of land, one hundred and sixty acres, in the northeast corner of section 17, township 7 North, range 10 East which after consulting a plat map of the county I determined to be exactly where the original downtown of Tyronza lay. This had to be the same person. Martha Stalker and M.A. Stocker were one and the same. I checked marriage records for the county but could locate no licenses for Duncan Stocker or Stalker and Martha anyone. I needed to go back to the census for more clues.

I pulled up the census record again, printing it out so I could carry it with me on all future trips. It was at that time that I realized how much I had missed the first time I looked at it. I was so excited to find a record for the person I thought I was looking for that I forgot to take notice of other information that might help me. According to the census record, Martha was forty-two years old at the time of the census. The census page was dated June 25, 1880 which would place her birth (if the age was correct and most times I have learned that it is not) sometime between June 26, 1837 and June 25, 1838. She was also reported to have been born in Arkansas, which was interesting since Arkansas had entered the union as the 25th state on June 15, 1836. According to the census report, both of her parents were born in Arkansas as well. This meant that the family was in the state when it was the Territory of Arkansas, and possibly even earlier. Her marital status was that of a widow and her occupation was keeping house. She could neither read nor write.

Her four children shared three surnames, Baker, Pittman, and Stocker, which indicated that she had possibly been married as many as three times although there could be several reasons for the multiple surnames. The older child, James Baker, could have been born out of wedlock and might bear her maiden name. The older daughter could be married or widowed and could bear her husband's surname. James was twenty-one and a farmer, born in Arkansas and his father was shown to have been born in Tennessee. He could read, but not write. The second child was an eighteen-year-old daughter listed as N.C. Pittman. The census indicated that she was single, which ruled out Pittman as a married name since she would have been recorded as either married, divorced, or widowed if that were the case. Her father had been born in Mississippi, which also pointed to a different father. She had no occupation and was not attending school. The other two children, both girls, were named Julia F. and Mary E., ages ten and four, and both carried the surname Stocker. They were born in Arkansas and their father, presumably Duncan, was shown to be a Canadian. The final member of the household was the hired man, J.H. Rushing, a native of Tennessee, aged thirty-two. His parents were both born in Tennessee which ruled out the possibility that he was a brother of Martha's as both of her parents were from Arkansas. He was listed on the census as a veteran, most likely of the Civil War but which side he fought for was not listed.[200]

This was a good start with some valuable clues. Since Julia's birthplace was Arkansas and she was ten years old, the family should be listed in the 1870 census for Arkansas. I checked for Stockers and Stalkers but could not locate them. This is not uncommon for the time period. The 1870 enumeration occurred shortly after the end of the American Civil War when life in eastern Arkansas was difficult to say the least. There was also controversy surrounding the 1870 census as population growth nationwide was not as strong as it was thought it should be. New York and Pennsylvania officials complained so bitterly that the president, Ulysses S. Grant, ordered a recount of those states. The final bit of information I took from the 1880 census was this: According to the dates on the pages that were recorded by the census taker, Martha and her family had been counted on June 25th, a Friday. The last families that he had visited had been counted on June 22nd, a Tuesday. Therefore they were a three day journey across the swamps from the last residents of the county he had visited which underscored how very remote the place was at the time.

I looked for the family in the 1860 federal enumeration, first looking for Duncan, since the two should not have been married to each other at this time, based on the probable birth dates for her two older children. Duncan seemed easier since I was not certain what name I would find Martha under. Surprisingly he turned up twice in the same census listed under the last name Stalker in neighboring Crittenden County. He was married at the time to a woman named Elizabeth, the mother of three children all bearing the last name Pearson, the youngest only a year old. The first enumeration finds him at

---

[200] Tennessee, like Arkansas, was greatly divided in its loyalties during the Civil War. Arkansas supplied over 10,000 troops to the Union Army during the war, outnumbered only by Tennessee. See Thomas A. DeBlack, *With Fire and Sword: Arkansas, 1861-1874*, (Fayetteville: University of Arkansas Press), 2003, 31.

Edmondson post office, Proctor Township, Crittenden County and employed as a sawyer in a lumber mill. He was twenty-seven years old, born in Canada to Canadian born parents. That count took place on June 15, 1860. On July 9 of the same year, Duncan and Elizabeth are again enumerated, living in Mound City, along the river in Hopefield Township, Crittenden County. Duncan was listed as a laborer but the rest of the information is the same. The couple apparently moved and ended up being counted in both places.

Since Crittenden County and the area around present day Marion and West Memphis was one of the earliest settled areas in the state, I decided to see if I could find any Pittmans or Bakers in the county. My search brought up a Martha Pittman living in Jackson Township in the Edmondson post office.[201] She is twenty-two years old and born in Arkansas and married to David Pittman, a twenty-two-year-old farmer, born in Mississippi. That agreed with the 1880 census information for the daughter N.C. Pittman whose father was born in Mississippi. There is a two-year-old son in the home named James who was the same age and name as Martha Stocker's son, James Baker. Also in the house is a twenty-five-year-old woman named Caroline Lewis. She was also born in Arkansas. My first assumption was that she could be a sister to Martha, resulting in a possible birth surname, as the birthplace information for the parents of both matched, but it was going to take some work to prove it.

From here I checked the Crittenden County Courthouse in Marion to search for marriage licenses for Martha and her husbands, which I knew to be Duncan and David Pittman and possibly someone named Baker. I turned up nothing for Duncan and Martha, but did locate a license for Duncan and Elizabeth. They were married on June 3, 1860, less than two

---

[201] Edmondson was also the post office given for Duncan and Elizabeth in the first census listing, but in Proctor Township. The Edmondson post office apparently served a very large population of western Crittenden County at that time.

weeks prior to the first census enumeration they appeared in. I also discovered a license dated January 3, 1860 between David A. Pittman and Mrs. Martha Ann Baker. That information answered two questions; first that she was married to James's father, and second what her full given name was. A further search of the marriage records turned up the earlier marriage, this time between J.L. Baker and Miss Martha A. Lewis on 5 March, 1857. Now I had her birth surname and a good timeline of events for her early married life, except I still could not find the marriage to Duncan. Plus, definitely knowing that she was a Lewis made the connection to Caroline Lewis more plausible.

I went back to the internet to look at an online map site that traces the county and state border changes over the history of the state.[202] Martha and David lived in Jackson Township which bordered Poinsett, Cross, and St. Francis Counties. There were parts of the eastern portion of Crittenden County that had been transferred to both St. Francis and Cross Counties in 1873. With shifting borders and with the swampy terrain that existed in the area at the time, it was possible that Duncan and Martha obtained a license in one of the other counties which would require trips to both the St. Francis County Courthouse in Forrest City and the Cross County Courthouse in Wynne, as I had already searched in Poinsett County. Of course, it is possible that the record could lie elsewhere as the American population was as mobile in many respects then as they are now.

Since the only male in her family in 1880 was her older child, I looked online at *Ancestry.com* to see if James Baker was listed in the 1900 census enumeration and to see if he was still living in Tyronza. I chose him because his surname would not

---

[202] The map referenced is at located at <http://www.arkansas.n2genealogy.com/ar-maps.html>. This is a fascinating website which features an animated map showing state and county boundary changes from 1813 until the county boundaries were finalized in 1925.

change with marriage like the girls very likely would have by that time. I could not locate him there or anywhere in the state, but that was not unusual as many men moved on with the railroad, the timber camps, or some other money-making scheme. A name like his, with both the given and surnames being very common, would prove difficult to trace as well. I gave up on that track for the time, at least until I could learn more about him.

While looking at the border changes on the internet, I decided to do a simple search on *Google.com* for Martha Stalker with no results. I went back to *Ancestry.com* and completed a search of the overall database for Martha Stalker. The site is a family history website that contains not only digital copies of official records but charts and records compiled by individuals about their own families and stored and shared with other researchers. This time I received a hit on a book titled, *The Descendants of David Anthony Pittman: Seven Generations*. Could this be the David Pittman she was married to? The book was a self-published affair finished in 1981 by a man named Roger Haley Howard and it was not available at that time at the Arkansas State University library.[203] The author's surname, Howard, is a common name in Tyronza history so I began doing a variety of online searches, again using *Google.com* as my search engine, for the name Howard and Tyronza. I located a webpage recording the interments in the Tyronza Cemetery for Marcus R. Howard and Nancy Caroline Howard. Nancy Caroline Howard could be N.C. Pittman. Her year of birth was listed as 1863 which would reasonably coincide with the 1880 census (1862-1863) and the dates of her parents' marriage in 1860. I did another online[204] search for

---

[203] I could find the book in only one library at the time, the William F. Laman Library in North Little Rock. A copy of the book has now been placed in the Arkansas State University Archives by Mrs. Stalker's descendants.

[204] All internet searches were completed using *Google.com*, unless otherwise noted.

Nancy Caroline Howard and came up with another cemetery database, this time for the Whitton Cemetery in neighboring Mississippi County but very close to Tyronza. Buried there in an unmarked grave were William Cornelius Perkins, born in 1857 and died 26 December, 1888, and a note showing that he was the first husband of Nancy Caroline Howard and that they had married in Mississippi County on 20 February, 1881. The note also explained that she had married Marcus Aurelius Howard on 6 January, 1890 in Crittenden County. Buried in an adjacent plot, also in an unmarked grave was the mother of Nancy Caroline Howard, Martha Ann Stalker.

Part of my mystery was solved, but the more I learned about this woman and her family, the more I wanted to know. She fascinated me like no other person in the town, and I decided to see how much I could learn about her life. After all, she lived during the period of Tyronza's history in which there is the least amount of data that was easily accessible. She had been there from the beginning of the town's settlement, and according to the cemetery website had died in 1903. That placed her right in the middle of the early years of the town when Tyronza grew from a railroad camp gravel pit in the early 1880s, through its time as a timber camp, and into the era of the small farm. She had witnessed it all.

Since one of the first places I found her name was in Edward Palmer's journal, I assumed that perhaps she had operated a boarding house of some sort. That may have been a bit of a stretch because he was digging in the mounds on her land. But since the railroad had built their tracks, depot, and gravel pit, all in the center of her property, what better place for all of them to set up shop than in her parlor? She was a single woman on her own in the middle of nowhere. How was she supposed to support herself? At this point I finally took the time to search for James extensively in the census records from 1900 onward and did not locate him anywhere. Did he die as Duncan had, or had he eventually left the area for greener pastures elsewhere? I believed he had died in Tyronza because

Palmer had noted that there were two mounds that Mrs. Stalker had asked him not to dig on. One was the one on which her home sat and where she said she brought her livestock during times of overflow, and the second was a smaller mound located slightly northwest of her home where he recorded there were white settlers' graves. Something told me that these were the final resting places of Duncan and James, but I had no way to be certain. She and some of the railroad workers had reported to Palmer that numerous graves belonging to the Indians had been disturbed when they built the right of way up for the tracks to rest on, but they had left this mound untouched, and according to Palmer's map it lay directly alongside the railroad tracks where it would have been easy to access for fill.

I moved forward by looking at the next logical place for Martha, which was the 1900 federal census.[205] I found her, still living in Tyronza with a nine-year-old boy, Jesse Hudson who was listed as her grandson, and a boarder named Matilda Rushing. Since daughter Nancy had married a Perkins and a Howard, this little boy must be the child of one of the two younger daughters. Apparently, at least the mother, Martha's daughter, was dead at the time and maybe the father. I located Nancy and her family living not far from Martha with her husband Marcus Howard, who was engaged in farming. I created a spreadsheet to record all of the residents in Tyronza Township at the time and found no one whose name or date of birth corresponded with either Julia or Mary, and no one else

---

[205] The 1890 Federal Census was partially destroyed by a fire at the National Archives in 1921. One quarter of the total was completely burned and approximately fifty percent was damaged by smoke and water. In December of 1932, the Librarian of Congress approved destruction of the badly damaged records believing them too far gone to save. That enumeration is particularly interesting as it was the first to be tabulated electronically using punch cards and a tabulating machine.

with the surname Hudson. What had happened to the other children?[206]

Researching women in history is a difficult undertaking, especially in a remote area like this one. In a paternalistic society like ours, women were and often still are, relegated to second class citizen status. Aside from the missing son James Baker, Martha Stalker was in a family of women. Everything I knew about her involved females. She had three daughters and I believed a sister. I had to know who the men were and more about them to move ahead. Women generally take on the husband's surname after marriage, and in that day and time, everything that the family owned was considered the property of the husband. Although Arkansas was one of the few states that allowed a woman to own land in her own right, I still had to know the names of the men in her life to proceed, and not just husbands' names but neighbors' and in-laws', as her surname had changed several times and with the name changes came changes in her life. I had no idea how much her life had transformed with each name change, but I was soon to find out.

One of the best web-based sources for genealogical and local history work in the states west of the Mississippi River is the Office of Land Management's General Land Office site.[207] The General Land Office maintained the records for those seeking land through military service and homesteading the public

---

[206] The 1900 census recorded for statistical purposes how many children each woman had given birth to and how many currently survived. Martha Stalker had given birth to six children and only two currently survived. One was obviously Nancy Caroline. I believed that James was probably dead by this time since I could not find him anywhere. This left one of the two younger children as the other survivor.

[207] The website is at www.glorecords.com and contains not only individual homestead applications but also the original plat maps of each section and range in Arkansas. I also located the original 1819 plat map for the section and range that would later include Tyronza which provided an interesting look at the place shortly after the 1811-12 earthquakes and before it was altered so extensively by humans in the early twentieth century.

domain lands which was a popular manner of obtaining property in northeast Arkansas. By entering a section, range, and meridian a researcher can obtain a list of all of the applications for homesteads filed there. Tyronza is located in section 10, range 7 of the 5th principal meridian and the search proved lucrative. Among the listings were three that were of interest. The first was for James Baker who had homesteaded one hundred sixty acres adjoining the land that Martha Stalker owned on the south side and which would include the town of Tyronza from Church Street almost to the town cemetery. I pulled up the digital image of the homestead certificate awarded in 1890. It stated that the certificate was being awarded to the heirs of James Baker, deceased. Unless James had married between 1880 and his death, which would have occurred prior to 1890, then his heirs would most likely include his mother. A second certificate of interest was for Thomas J. Hudson and included land located south of Tyronza in section 29. An online inspection of his certificate indicated that his land had been claimed by his heirs in 1898 as he was deceased. If this was Jesse Hudson's father then he was probably the only heir and as his grandmother appeared to be his guardian, she may have filed the claim. The third claim of interest involved Rhoda Carroll whose land lay directly south of that homesteaded by James Baker. In the 1880 census the family living closest to the Stalker family was the John and Rhoda Carroll family. Her application was dated 1889 and was assigned to her as the widow of John Carroll. John Carroll's name was of interest as the Tyronza City Cemetery contains an Indian mound in the northeast corner which had three old stones on it. I had determined that these three were in fact the three oldest marked graves in the cemetery. One of them is that of Silas Lafayette Carroll, son of J. and R.C. Carroll. The 1880 census confirmed that Silas was the son of John and Rhoda.[208]

---

[208] I have subsequently learned that the double mound in the back corner of

The search for the woman I now thought of as Tyronza's founding mother was a first-rate mystery and one that consumed a large amount of my time and efforts. Every new detail learned about her life brought up a new question. The search required every bit of detective knowledge I had managed to acquire over my years in law enforcement and the best of my genealogical skills, but I felt compelled to continue. There was something about this woman and her family that pulled me to keep looking for clues and working to find answers.

In the spring of 2010, I got an opportunity to visit the only library I could find that had a copy of Roger Haley Howard's book on David Anthony Pittman and his descendants. As I stated earlier, western civilization is primarily a male-centered society and the Pittman book illustrated that clearly. First the title, *The Descendants of David Anthony Pittman: Seven Generations*, hints at a life that was long and full, with many children and possibly many wives to bear them. That could not have been farther from the truth. David Anthony Pittman was married one time to our Martha Ann, fathered one child, the girl Nancy Caroline, and died at the ripe old age of twenty-four. In the book that told his own life story he is dead by the time the reader turns to page two. The title could have just as easily included his wife's name as all of the descendants were hers as well, and could have begun with his daughter but it did not. They were only sidelines in his story even though they outlived him by forty and ninety-one years respectively, and the bulk of what happened to the family was lived out by them. While Howard, one of Martha Ann Stalker's great-grandsons, focused more on the men in his past, he included enough tidbits for me to flesh out the story of his female ancestors, and what a story they had.

---

the Tyronza Cemetery was originally called the Webber Cemetery, as the land was provided by Benjamin F. Webber, another of the Stalker family neighbors in 1880. There are numerous unmarked graves located on the mounds belonging to the Webber and Carroll families.

I learned from Howard that females in the Lewis family did not often use their first given name. Mrs. Stalker and her daughters, the women I had referred to for the past four years as Martha, Nancy, Julia, and Mary, all used their middle names exclusively except when signing official documents. They were better known to their friends and family members as Ann, Caroline, Florence, and Ella, a bit of information once learned which helped to clarify the search for them in the records.[209] It also required me to rethink who they were in my mind as they all had new names and had existed to me the other way for so long that it was difficult to think of them in any other manner. Roger Howard focused his efforts on the family of Caroline and her second husband, Marcus Aurelius Howard as that was his direct ancestral line, but included her Perkins descendants as well, and included enough information on others in the family that I was able to develop the descent charts for Ann's other children to some extent.

James Baker, known as Jimmy, died young. He homesteaded the one hundred sixty acre parcel of land that now lies on the west side of Main Street and south of Church Street in 1881 where he had begun clearing land to farm. He was engaged to be married to an unknown young woman when he died of a fever on December 23, 1881. His mother completed the homestead and added his land to her holdings.[210]

Julia Florence Stalker had married Thomas Jefferson Hudson in 1889. Tom was a native of Kentucky where he grew up with his childhood friend, Marcus Howard. Tom Hudson first

---

[209] Ella Stalker Thorp was in the 1900 Federal Census enumeration for Tyronza, living between her mother and half-sister Caroline. I had not found her originally as I was looking for a woman named Mary.

[210] Martha Ann Stalker, Testimony of Claimant to fulfill the Homestead Application for The Heirs of James Baker, 25 August, 1888, General Land Office, Bureau of Land Management, National Archives, Washington, DC. The testimony filed by Ann Stalker reports that her hired man, John Rushing had built a log cabin on the property where she lived at times, and also rented out to the schoolteacher. She grew cotton and corn on the property and kept pigs.

traveled to the swamps of northeast Arkansas to obtain work in the timber industry where he met Florence, maybe while staying at her mother's boarding house. He encouraged his friend Marc to come to Arkansas where there was not only work, but a sister of Florence's that he thought Marc might be interested in. Marc made the trip, where he reported to his grandson Roger, that he did find work and a wife as well.[211] The full homestead application for the eighty-acre parcel of land homesteaded by Thomas Jefferson Hudson in 1890 and fulfilled by his heirs, namely Martha Ann Stalker, guardian of his minor child Jesse Hudson in 1898, record that Tom died in 1891 and Florence in 1892.[212] Ann paid two hundred dollars to the Poinsett County Court as a bond to assume legal guardianship of her two-year-old grandson.[213]

Another of Ann Stalker's great grandsons, Thomas Perkins of Forrest City, Arkansas, happened to visit the Southern Tenant Farmers Museum in 2009 and we have corresponded fairly regularly since that time. Through discussions with him and using bits and pieces of interviews with two of Caroline's daughters that were conducted in the 1980s by Roger Howard, I have been able to learn more about Ann and her family. Ann Stalker did indeed run a boarding house that she opened when the railroad started working on the roadbed in the early 1880s. The daughters worked alongside her. The hours would have been long, hot, and busy but the boarding house allowed her to finally achieve a measure of financial independence.

Mary Ella Stalker married John Edward Thorp at Tyronza in 1893. The couple moved to Jonesboro where John died in 1912.

---

[211] Roger Haley Howard included in his book transcripts of two interviews that he did with his grandparents, Mark and Caroline Howard, at their home near Tyronza on Christmas Day, 1939.

[212] Thomas Jefferson Hudson's land lay just south of the Cherry Beam Church and Cemetery which borders the property on the north and is now part of the Norcross land.

[213] Martha Ann Stalker, Testimony of Claimant, Homestead Application for The Heirs of Thomas J. Hudson, 12 June 1897, General Land Office, Bureau of Land Management, National Archives, Washington, DC.

Ella moved to Memphis and spent the rest of her life there. She died in 1950 and was buried in the Jonesboro City Cemetery. I have corresponded with her great grandson Scott Williams, but he knows little of the family history on this line. John and Ella were partners with Ann in a real estate venture in Tyronza. They platted J.E. Thorp's First Addition to the Town of Tyronza in the mid 1890s and began selling Ann's old farm off a lot at a time to the new families that were arriving set upon making Tyronza their home. Included among the buyers were John A. Emrich who purchased five acres from the group and built a house, barn, and other outbuildings, and according to George Beley, the first structure that housed the Tyronza General Supply.

Ann had at least two sisters, Caroline and Paralee, and a brother named Dallas. Caroline was older and Paralee was believed to be younger. Dallas's age is unknown. I have yet to locate Ann's parents as it appears that they died prior to 1860 leaving fairly young children. A sixteen-year-old whose name was recorded by the census taker as Perla Lewis was living a few doors away from Ann and David in 1860 with a John and Lucinda Stanley family. Lucinda is too young to be Ann, Caroline, and Paralee's mother, but I think I can assume that this young woman Perla, is Paralee based on correspondence between John Stanley and David's mother, who was also named Nancy Caroline Pittman. Mrs. Pittman received a letter from John Stanley in 1863 that discusses in some detail the deaths of her husband and son at the hands of Confederate guerillas in December, 1862.[214] Mr. Stanley mentions both Ann and the baby Caroline and states that Dallas is living with her now. Dallas was mentioned again in discussing his report to

---

[214] According to Roger Haley Howard, the family letters concerning the Pittman families Civil War experiences were in the hands of Pittman descendant, LaQuita June Braden Montgomery of Andrews, Texas in the early 1980s. The whereabouts of the documents since that time are unknown.

Mrs. Pittman that a soldier named Dority[215] had been seen with the horses belonging to her husband and son and he believed he was the one responsible for their deaths. Stanley obviously had intimate knowledge of the family which would indicate that Perla is again Paralee. Ann's father-in-law and brother-in-law were killed by Confederate guerillas somewhere in Arkansas after they returned from service in the Union Army and their bodies buried and cared for until after the war when they were retrieved and taken back to the family home in Independence County. I strongly believed that Ann was the person who did this service and am convinced now that is the case.

Caroline disappears from the records after her 1860 mention in the census in David and Ann's home. Tom Perkins told me that she married a man named John W. Roman and had two daughters, Cash and Mary. Cash married James Wesley (J.W.) Hood who hailed from the Gibson's Bayou area north of Earle in Crittenden County. She died young and is buried in an unmarked grave at the Hood Cemetery in Crittenden County. Mary married George Washington Hays and also died young after she was crushed by her horse in a fall. Cash and J.W.'s marriage bond records her name as C.A. Cook at her marriage. The 1880 census for Crittenden County records that John W. Roman was living in Tyronza Township with his new wife Z. Roman, his nine-year-daughter Mary and one-year-old son, L.C. Since Cash is not mentioned in the family record she may not be John's daughter and may be living with another family member. Cook may be her birth surname or a surname from an earlier marriage but I have yet to determine that. Caroline Lewis Roman is obviously dead by 1880. An interesting aside is that after Edward Palmer left Tyronza Station where he worked on Ann Stalker's land recording the mounds, he traveled off the path he had chosen along the railroad line, to look at some mounds he had been told about on the John

---

[215] Most likely a misspelling of a name such as Dougherty or Doherty.

Roman farm in Crittenden County.[216] Undoubtedly this is the same man as Ann's brother-in-law and she was most likely the informant for Palmer and leads me to believe that the families remained close even after Caroline's death. Ann's daughter Caroline was also known to ride her horse to the church at Gibson's Bayou on regular visits to attend services and visit with family.[217] In an interesting aside, several of Caroline Lewis Roman's descendants played a part in the activities directed against the Southern Tenant Farmers Union in the Earle and Parkin area including being a part of the mob that captured Howard Kester and Evelyn Smith at a church near Earle. This mob almost lynched Kester before forcing the pair to drive to West Memphis where they retained the couple's car and forced them to walk to safety across the Harahan Bridge back to Memphis.[218]

Dallas is reported by one of Caroline's daughters to have married a young woman named Febia, which I believe may be the name Phoebe. I can locate no one with any semblance of those names in the area at any time but they seem to be well known among the family so I assume they were living close enough for regular contact. Dallas, like his female family members may have used his middle name as well, which compounds the difficulty in locating him. It was Paralee that gave me much trouble in trying to locate her whereabouts but once I made the connection, many of the riddles of both Ann

---

[216] Marvin D. Jeter and Dan F. Morse, ""Nearly Distroyed": Palmer's Last Work in Northeast Arkansas, Late 1883", in *Edward Palmer's Arkansaw Mounds*, Marvin D. Jeter, ed., Tuscaloosa: University of Alabama Press, 1990, p. 345. John Roman's land was located very near the Gibson's Bayou area along the Tyronza River.

[217] Caroline Pittman Perkins Howard was with Mary Roman Hayes when she was injured in the accident with the horse. The horse was apparently spooked by something and in an attempt to get away threw Mary and then fell across her legs, crushing them. She never walked again.

[218] See the letter from H.L. Mitchell to Prosecuting Attorney Denver L. Dudley, in *A Documentary History of Arkansas*, (Fayetteville: University of Arkansas Press), 1984, 208.

Stalker's life and maybe even some surrounding Tyronza itself seemed to open up.

Tom Perkins told me personally on at least two occasions, and Roger Howard's book concurred, that Paralee had married first a Mr. Mullins and then a Mr. Wilkins. Neither man could remember their given names though. I found a footnote that I had missed in my first reading of the book which indicated that Paralee Mullins was buried in the Dead Timber Cemetery,[219] the same place as her sister Ann. The 1880 census, where I had first located Ann and her children, records that one of the four families who lived in close proximity was that of Jasper and Roenia Mullins. I wondered if Paralee had maybe married one of their sons but the couple was a few years younger than Duncan and Ann so that most likely was not the case. I searched for Jasper's family thinking that maybe Paralee had married one of his brothers, but I found that his family had never come into the region staying at their home in Independence County near Oil Trough. An Arkansas History Commission web search showed that Roenia P. Mullins of Poinsett County had applied for a Confederate widow's pension in 1926 and I made a trip to Little Rock to look at the record. It yielded one bit of information that seemed very strange. Jasper N. Mullins had died in 1882. Why had his widow waited forty-four years to apply for his pension? The answer lay partially in the fact that the State of Arkansas did not sanction widow's pensions until 1915, but that did not explain the additional eleven year gap. There was no information on her children that would help with the connection to Paralee.

A search for a Mr. Wilkins yielded no results either. A check of some notes I had taken after a visit with Tom Perkins resulted in another clue that I had failed to notice. Tom told me that Paralee had three children, two boys named James and Charles Mullins and a daughter named Lee Wilkins. I

---

[219] Dead Timber Cemetery is now known as the Whitton Cemetery.

searched *Ancestry.com* for James Mullins and located a James O. Mullins on a World War I draft enrollment. He was married and farming for John A. Emrich near Tyronza. His date of birth confirmed that he was born in 1878 in Arkansas. A search for James O. Mullins in the 1880 census for Poinsett County, turned up J.O. Mullins, the son of Jasper N. and R.P. Mullins. I gave that particular census another thorough review and discovered four sons, J.W., age 13; C.E., age 12; J.O., age 2; and John William, age 5 months. There was also a nine-year-old nephew named R. Barnes. C.E. could certainly be Charles. The 1900 and 1910 Tyronza census records confirmed that C.E. and J.O. were indeed Charles E. and James O. Mullins.

There was no sign though of a girl named Lee or of either of the other boys listed in 1880. I tried a search for Lee Wilkins, using the second husband's surname, in the 1900 census and found her living in Cave City, Sharp County, Arkansas with her parents S.B. and R.P. Wilkins. A boarder named Robert Barnes, age thirty, was also in the home. Robert Barnes was most likely R. Barnes, the nine-year-old nephew living in the Mullins home in 1880. Roenia Paralee Mullins Wilkins was Paralee Lewis, using her middle name like her sister and nieces.[220] She was there under my nose the whole time and I had not thought to put the clues together. Cave City was also the town that Ann's daughter Caroline moved to after Ann's death so her children could attend high school. I always wondered why she had chosen Cave City as her school of choice when there were other high schools closer to Tyronza and now that there was a family connection there, it all made perfect sense. What I discovered next was, I believe, maybe the

---

[220] The discovery of yet another member of the family who used a middle name instead of their first name also may explain why I have been unable to find Ann and Paralee's other siblings, Caroline and Dallas. Caroline had given that name in the 1860 census and Ann had given her name as Martha. Caroline may have used a middle name as well that I have been unable to find. The brother may also be using a middle name. He is referred to in letters and family memory as Dallas, but that may not have been his first name confusing my search for him.

key to not only my fascination with Ann Stalker, but the whole mystery surrounding the history of Tyronza. It may very well center not on Ann, but on her third husband, Duncan.

The American Civil War holds great fascination for me but I was relieved at the thought that I need not bother with research into that era in Arkansas history as the town of Tyronza had not existed in any form during that time period. The history of the war has long been told in stories of epic battles with heroic generals leading unnamed men in gallant charges across now sacred ground. While that is beginning to change and the rest of the story is starting to come forward, the story of the war in Arkansas is dark, difficult, and confusing. Noted military historian and West Point faculty member Major Robert Mackey has stated that the war in Arkansas was the most perfect example of guerilla warfare ever waged. It took its toll on the people and the land and many changed their loyalties during the four years of the war. The Delta side of the Ridge was only sparsely populated at the time with settlement scattered up and down the various rivers such as the St. Francis and the Tyronza. Ann Stalker had lived through the war in neighboring Crittenden County as the widow of a Union soldier or at the least a Union sympathizer. Her story was made more intriguing after she married a Confederate veteran after the war's close.

Duncan Stalker and his friend Jasper Mullins had served together as elite Confederate cavalrymen for three years. During the American Civil War, young men from towns and counties would join the army together forming companies with names relative to their home. Their company, the Crittenden Rangers, was such a unit. The Rangers were formed during a recruiting drive at the county seat of Marion on April 13, 1861, while Rebel artillery under Confederate General P.G.T. Beauregard was still firing at Fort Sumter. The *Memphis Daily Appeal* in its April 17, 1861 issue ran a notice of the company's creation and a second article with the text of the flag ceremony held the same day at Hopefield.[221] The company was equipped by a two thousand dollar appropriation from the Crittenden County Court which was to pay for horses and saddles, the state was to provide arms, and the citizens of the county were raising funds to purchase pistols. It is important to note that at the time of the unit's organization, Arkansas had yet to leave the Union. The County Court had issued tax payer money to fund a military unit that was forming to fight against the government of the United States from which the State of Arkansas had yet to withdraw. Secession had been a difficult issue in Arkansas with the voters electing not to secede early in 1861, but choosing delegates from each county to represent them at a secession convention to be held in March in Little Rock. The final vote was sharply divided with the mountain section of the state highly opposed to leaving the federal union. The delegates failed to pass an ordinance of secession on the first attempt. The initiative was taken up for the second time by the convention on the 6th day of May and passed by a vote of fifty-nine to one.[222] The Crittenden Rangers enlisted in the service of the State of Arkansas on June 3, 1861 and rode off to join the garrison at Pitman's Ferry near Pocahontas on the Current River.

In June of that year, the Confederate government appointed William J. Hardee a brigadier general and placed him in control of troops at Pitman's Ferry. His job was to convert the state troops in Arkansas to regular Confederate Army service, something many of the Arkansans were not happy about. They feared that by joining the Confederate Army they would

---

[221] The *Memphis Daily Appeal* article was located in the Chronicling America historic newspaper collection at the Library of Congress on page 3, column 2. <http://chroniclingamerica.loc.gov/lccn/sn83045160/1861-04-17/ed-1/seq-3/>

[222] Michael B. Dougan, *Confederate Arkansas: The People and Politics of a Frontier State in Wartime* (Tuscaloosa: University of Alabama Press, 1976), 63., and Thomas A. DeBlack, *With Fire and Sword: Arkansas, 1861-1874*, (Fayetteville: University of Arkansas Press, 2003) 28.

be forced to leave Arkansas. Troops were offered a chance to enlist in the regular army or receive a discharge and many accepted the latter rather than leave their family behind. Major Calvin Collier, in his history of the 3rd Arkansas Cavalry notes that the men who made up the unit held no political belief except the one that allowed a state to join or leave the Union at will. They fought for Arkansas and Arkansas only.[223] This idea was made all the more interesting by the fact that the unit spent almost its entire period of service in the regular Confederate Army fighting outside the state.

The unit was initially incorporated into Company C of 6th Battalion Arkansas Cavalry and placed in the 1st (Hardee's) Division of the Army of Central Kentucky where they saw action in two skirmishes. Part of General Hardee's duty was to continue actively recruiting in Arkansas. A native of Georgia, he enlisted the assistance of a well-known Arkansas politician by the name of Thomas Carmichael Hindman, who himself had obtained a commission in the Confederate Army as a brigadier general in command of a brigade of the Army of Mississippi. A fiery politician, Hindman had helped to secure the election of Henry Rector as governor in 1860 and assisted with putting down the ruling political dynasty in Arkansas known as The Family. He had hoped to be elected to the Confederate Congress but was denied a seat by the state legislature.[224]

Among the recruits that Hindman could count on were Duncan Stalker and Jasper Mullins who both enlisted at Marion on March 20, 1862 and joined the Crittenden Rangers immediately. Within three weeks of joining the army, the two

---

[223] Maj. Calvin L. Collier, USAF (Ret.), *The War Child's Children: A Story of the Third Arkansas Cavalry*. (Little Rock: Pioneer Press, 1965), 1.

[224] DeBlack, 29. Hindman was known for his fiery temperament and it was suggested that the Arkansas legislature feared he would lead the Confederate Congress down a radical path. Born in Mississippi he left the state after he challenged Col. William C. Falker (great grandfather of author William Faulkner) to a duel. An acquaintance stated that Hindman had "a wonderful talent for getting into fusses."

saw their first major action at the Battle of Shiloh. A short two weeks later, the 6th was consolidated with the 2nd Arkansas Cavalry Battalion to form the 2nd Arkansas Cavalry Regiment with the Crittenden Rangers forming the new Company B. They saw extensive action in Tennessee and Mississippi and fought in the First Battle of Corinth in May of 1862. The company was transferred a final time in January 1863 and become the new Company E of the 3rd Regiment Arkansas Cavalry. Duncan and Jasper were involved in extensive fighting as part of the famed Confederate Army of Tennessee. Their exploits would constitute a separate book entirely. They both survived, apparently unscathed until the end of the war, and surrendered with the remnants of the Army of Tennessee at Bennett Place near Durham, North Carolina.[225]

Shortly after the two left for Shiloh, back home in Arkansas the war had taken a horrible turn. On March 8, 1862, two weeks before Duncan and Jasper enlisted, Major General Earl Van Dorn, then the commander of the Confederate Army of the West, lost the Battle of Pea Ridge in northwest Arkansas. That loss coupled with the threat to the Army of Tennessee across the Mississippi River forced the Confederate leadership to have to decide between giving up Arkansas or losing Tennessee. Then as now, Arkansas was thought of in many circles, including many in the Confederate government in Richmond, as a poor country cousin, a backward place with few resources other than fighting men.[226] They chose to keep Tennessee. Van Dorn was ordered to move toward Shiloh with the bulk of his troops. As he left Arkansas, he emptied warehouses of necessary supplies, burned bridges, and destroyed the telegraph line between Little Rock and Fort

---

[225] For a fascinating look at the exploits of the 3rd Arkansas during the war see Maj. Calvin L. Collier, USAF (Ret.), *The War Child's Children: A Story of the Third Arkansas Cavalry,* (Little Rock: Pioneer Press), 1965.
[226] DeBlack, *With Fire and Sword,* 35, and Robert R. Mackey, *The Uncivil War: Irregular Warfare in the Upper South, 1861-1865,* (Norman: University of Oklahoma Press, 2004), 26.

Smith. Arkansas Governor Henry Rector, fearing for the safety of the state's residents, wrote a letter to President Jefferson Davis threatening to take the state back into the federal union if it was left without protection from the approaching Union Army of the Southwest under the command of Brigadier General Samuel R. Curtis.[227] Davis responded by sending the man responsible for the enlistment of both Duncan and Jasper, Brigadier General Thomas Carmichael Hindman, to Arkansas to assume command of the newly created Army of the Trans-Mississippi which included not only Arkansas, but Missouri, Louisiana, Texas, and the Indian Territory (present-day Oklahoma).

While Governor Rector had been assured by the Confederate government that Arkansas had not been forever abandoned, Van Dorn understood that it had been. Upon leaving the state he took everything that he could carry and destroyed the rest. Hindman, who had been wounded at Shiloh, stopped on his way through Memphis where he seized every firearm that he could find and close to one million dollars in cash to pay his army. Unfortunately, he arrived to find no supplies, no logistical support, no communications system, and no army. The few remaining troops in the state had been placed under the command of one of Hindman's political enemies, Albert Pike, and moved to the Indian Territory.[228]

Hindman made the decision to win the war in Arkansas at all costs. In early June of 1862, he imposed martial law on the citizens of the state, began seizing supplies and munitions, and started enforcing conscription laws. His final step was the one that would bring the brunt of the war down upon the

---

[227] Mackey, *The Uncivil War*, 25.
[228] Ibid, 29. Pike was in charge of a sizable contingent of Native American soldiers. A former Indian Agent in Arkansas, he had been sent to the Indian Territory to bring the Indian Nations into the service of the Confederacy.

civilian population of Arkansas.[229] On June 17, 1862, Hindman issued General Order No. 17, which became known as The Bands of Ten Act. It instructed the people of Arkansas to organize themselves into independent companies of at least ten men, to elect a captain, lieutenant, and a sergeant, and to wage guerilla warfare against the Federal forces in any way they saw fit.[230]

Hindman apparently realized that the eventual outcome of his order might be chaos and followed it up almost immediately with General Order No. 18 which set up a command structure that the so-called independent bands were to follow. While the first order was published in every newspaper in the state and distributed widely, the second was less visible with most publications focusing only on martial law. One of General Curtis's officers, Colonel Graham Fitch wrote a letter to Hindman dated June 28, 1862 in which he stated, "Your captains of ten will soon become little else than highway banditti, more terrible to citizens of your own State than to soldiers and sailors of the United States." Unfortunately, his prophesy would prove correct. By August, Hindman had raised an irregular force of five thousand men. Historian Robert Mackey says that within a year, "Arkansas Confederates went from adherence to the laws of civilized warfare to an unrestrained guerilla conflict."[231]

The growing seasons of 1861 and 1862 were not good ones. Heavy spring rains followed by a hot and dry summer resulted in poor harvests. A round of cholera in the hog population also contributed to the decrease in food not only for the civilian population, but both Union and Confederate armies which were working in the state as well. To make matters worse, the state's planters continued to grow cotton as

---

[229] Memphis had fallen to the Union on June 6, 1862 after a two hour naval battle, leaving the Arkansas side of the river vulnerable to Union predations, especially Crittenden County just across the river.
[230] Ibid, 30.
[231] Ibid, 33.

a cash crop rather than focus their efforts on food for the people and the military. The Confederate state government in Little Rock attempted to stop the practice by imposing a thirty dollar per bale tax on cotton and limiting production to two acres per hand. The newspapers of the state begged growers to plant corn and wheat, but they were ignored.[232]

Hindman's Bands of Ten added to the food problems by constantly attacking and stealing the Union Army supply trains in an effort to curtail their efforts on the battlefield. Hindman's strategy worked in that Curtis's men were forced to spend the entire summer of 1862 foraging for food, but it also left the civilian population to suffer.[233] By the winter of 1862 and 1863, Hindman lost all control of the guerilla forces. Capt. Joseph F. Barton,[234] a local guerilla leader in Crittenden County wrote to Hindman to inform him that he was allowing his men to seize and sell Union property in order to keep them motivated.[235] The new Union commander in Memphis, Major General William T. Sherman, took a dim view of Hindman's guerilla approach to warfare and told him so in a letter dated September 28, 1862. Sherman writes, "You know full well that it is to the interest of the people of the South that we should not disperse our troops as guerillas; but at that game your guerillas would meet their equals, and the world would be shocked by the acts of atrocity resulting from such warfare." Sherman would capture and hang the guerillas as criminals

---

[232] DeBlack, *With Fire and Sword*, 73.
[233] Ibid, 34, and Mackey, *The Uncivil War*, 34.
[234] Muster records for the Crittenden Rangers record that Barton had been one of the charter members of the company, but he was not listed on the rolls of the company when it transferred to the regular Confederate Army. Apparently he was one of those who chose to take a discharge rather than leave the state to fight.
[235] Mackey, *The Uncivil War*, 37. Ann Stalker, who at that time would have been considered a Union supporter, told stories for the rest of her life about people she called 'invaders" raiding her home during the war to steal and plunder, cutting pillows and mattresses to look inside. The items she did not want taken or destroyed she kept in a cotton sack hidden down inside what she referred to as a "dug well" on the property.

rather than treat them as prisoners of war.[236] Remember that at this time, Ann Stalker was living in Crittenden County, married to a Union husband. Duncan's first wife Elizabeth, and her children were also presumably still living here as well. Both women were right in the middle of some of the most horrendous guerilla fighting in the state.

Hindman saved Arkansas for the Confederacy but alienated the leadership in Richmond as well as other Rebel commanders. In July of 1862, he was relieved of command of the Army of the Trans-Mississippi by Brigadier General Theophilus Holmes, and put in charge of the much smaller District of Arkansas. On December 7, 1862, Hindman led his troops against the troops of Union Brigadier General James Blunt at a little place called Prairie Grove in Washington County. Now considered the bloodiest day in the state's history, the two commanders fought to a draw but Hindman's Confederates withdrew under cover of darkness resulting in a strategic victory for Blunt. The loss ended any hope of saving either Arkansas or Missouri for the Confederacy and the regular Rebel Army all but abandoned the state. The Union Army maintained garrisons at a few sites but for the most part the citizens were left to suffer at the hands of the guerillas.[237]

By 1863, both Confederates and their Union counterparts spent most of their time in Arkansas fighting the guerillas. In order for this type of partisan warfare to work, those doing the fighting must have the support of the local population in some form. Some bands of men like the ones fighting in Arkansas needed food and protection when the armies came searching for them. Because of the divided loyalties in the state, it was easy for the bands to find the support they needed. The Union Army, determined to find a new way to counter the guerilla effort, decided to punish those who were aiding them. On February 18, 1863, Major General Stephen Hurlburt ordered

---

[236] Ibid, 34.
[237] Ibid, 36.

the Crittenden County village of Hopefield fired for harboring guerilas. The Union Army gave the residents one hour to gather their belongings and then set fire to everything.[238] The Confederates approached the situation differently with cavalry Colonel Joseph O. Shelby initially attempting to appeal to the guerillas' conscience, but when that failed he set out to hunt them down. Thinking he could maybe incorporate them into his own forces, he reported to his commander, Major General Sterling Price, that they were no more than "brigands" and gave up the idea. Shelby first attempted just to arrest them but his disgust at the work they had been doing overwhelmed him. He ordered one of his battalion commanders to "shoot them whenever found...not one of them is to be spared."[239] By the end of the war, in many sections of the state the Union Army had been transformed into the protector of the citizens, rather than the guerilla bands as had been envisioned by Hindman.[240] The guerillas at Hopefield were led by two notorious men, the aforementioned Captain Joseph F. Barton and Captain James H. McGehee[241] of neighboring St. Francis County. They terrorized Union

---

[238] David O. Demuth, "The Burning of Hopefield," *The Arkansas Historical Quarterly*, 36:3 (Summer, 1977), 127. Hopefield was one of the earliest settlements in the state, established in 1795, and was located directly across the river from what is now Mud Island and below Mound City which was the last known address of Duncan Stalker and his first wife, Elizabeth. Its location as the eastern terminus of the Memphis and Little Rock Railroad made it an important piece of the wartime puzzle. The rail yard had been converted to a Confederate Armory early in the war and even though all of its citizens had taken the Oath of Alliance to the Federal government in the summer of 1862, many of them were not honoring that pledge.
[239] Mackey, 39.
[240] Ibid, 49.
[241] McGehee and his brother, Shadrack Jarmon McGehee were like Barton, original members of the Crittenden Rangers whose names disappear from the roles after the unit was placed in regular Confederate service.

shipping on the Mississippi River and were the primary reason that Hopefield was burned.[242]

The war raged on for another two years. Arkansas citizens on both sides of the affair were left to fend for themselves with civil authorities in the state either unable or unwilling to serve. As happens during times such as this, feelings of helplessness brought about a desire for revenge not only for opposing viewpoints in the war, but for old wrongs that had been settled years earlier.[243] By 1864, legitimate economic activity had pretty much ended. Gristmills, sawmills, mines, factories, and artisans had closed for business for a variety of reasons. Crops rotted in the fields because there simply were not enough hands left to bring them in. Inflation made most of the items that were available too expensive to buy. Those locations with Federal garrisons nearby fared better, but isolated locations away from Army protection suffered greatly.[244]

By the end of the war Arkansas no longer resembled the place that Duncan Stalker and Jasper Mullins had left in 1862. Historians now estimate that as much as one-half the population of the state, both its black and white citizens, were either dead or had moved away. Horses, cattle, and mule populations were reduced by forty to fifty percent statewide. Property values decreased from $5.32 per acre before the war to $2.21 per acre at war's end and what remained was burned out, overgrown, and abandoned to nature in many cases.[245]

Duncan Stalker has remained more elusive than his wife Ann and her children. A Canadian by birth, I can locate nothing to indicate whether he traveled to Arkansas with any other members of his family, and have thus far been unable to

---

[242] Leo E. Huff, "Jayhawkers and Bushwackers in Northern Arkansas During the Civil War," in *The Arkansas Historical Quarterly*. 24:2 (Summer 1965), 133.
[243] Daniel E. Sutherland, "Guerillas: The Real War in Arkansas," in *Civil War Arkansas: Beyond Battles and Leaders*, Anne J. Bailey and Daniel E, Sutherland, eds. (Fayetteville: University of Arkansas Press, 2000), 137.
[244] DeBlack, 120.
[245] DeBlack, 144.

determine where in Canada he hailed from or who his parents were. Nor have I been able to figure out what became of his first wife and family. Elizabeth Pearson had apparently been married before and had three daughters when she married Duncan in 1860. By March of 1862, when Duncan enlisted in the Confederate Army and left Arkansas, it is very possible that she could have given birth to a child of his. Was she still living when he left the state? I still do not know. If she was, how did she and her children fare during the war? Their last known location was Mound City which was then located on the river and in the middle of fighting both military and partisan, and a short distance from the ill-fated Hopefield. Residents of that area went where they could find safety and some measure of security. Elizabeth and her girls were all born in Tennessee and may have returned to that side of the river, if they survived at all.

Although Duncan lived through the war and surrendered with the rest of the 3rd Arkansas in North Carolina he is not listed with the rest of the unit, which did include Jasper Mullins, on the list of parolees at the end of the war. In Collier's work on the 3rd Arkansas Cavalry, titled *The War Child's Children*, he notes that after surrender there was a group of forty-seven men from the 3rd Arkansas, including nine of the Crittenden Rangers, who escaped from Union custody and were captured in Athens, Georgia where they were eventually paroled. This group lists among its members a Pvt. Stayker.[246] I have searched the muster roles and find no one with a name that closely resembles that one except Duncan Stalker.[247] Where were they going and what were they planning to do? I have yet to find an answer for those questions.

---

[246] Collier, *The War Child's Children*, 137.
[247] In his original muster into the unit his name is listed as Duncan Stalker. When the unit is incorporated into the 3rd Arkansas in 1863, his name is listed on the muster role as Dunkin Stawker. Stayker is most likely another misspelling of his surname.

In the modern world there are many options for locating missing loved ones after a disaster, but we also understand that there are times when there may be no easy way to make contact. We experienced that as a nation recently after the terrorist attacks of September 11, 2001, and again after Hurricane Katrina struck the Gulf Coast. The American Civil War brought about the same type of situation but on a much grander scale and without the benefit of modern technology to make the finding easier. It is possible that both Duncan and his wife survived the war, only never to find each other again. In the 1880 Federal Census for Memphis, there is an Elizabeth Stalker living as a boarder in a home on Exchange Street. She is working as a seamstress and is listed as a widow. With her is a teenage daughter named Maggie Stalker, who works as a store clerk. The two women's ages approximately correlate to those of Duncan's wife and a daughter that she could have given birth to who was fathered by Duncan. Could they be a missing wife and child that Duncan came back to and never found? With this in mind one must wonder what Duncan's emotional state was when he returned to Crittenden County. Disappointment, depression, anger, rage? The economy was destroyed and those most affected by it were the landless poor like Duncan.

In the meantime, Ann remained in Crittenden County the widow of a Union veteran, but considering her location in a heavily Confederate part of the state, her lot would have been bleak. Daughter Caroline told her grandchildren stories of the war years and her early life with her mother and brother. One of these stories involved Ann's attempt at homesteading a piece of land for her small family to live on and the young woman and her children carrying a tent in which to live while they filed the claim. Was this when she moved to Poinsett County? According to documents signed by two of her closest neighbors and accompanying the homestead claim she filed on Jimmy's land in 1888, she moved to Poinsett County in

1867.²⁴⁸ Had she, alone with her children, settled on the mound in the swamp years before she and Duncan bought the land from Napoleon B. Martis? I believe that she did. So where did Duncan Stalker come from and how did he end up out in the swamps of Poinsett County? The answer I now believe lies in events that transpired after the war's end.

When the war began, Arkansas had a slave population approaching eleven thousand. At its conclusion, the number of African Americans still living within the borders of the state had fallen to approximately half that number. The very fabric of society had been ripped to shreds by the war. Dealing with the large number of freedmen compounded the already daunting project of rebuilding lives and the economy of the remaining white population. The Freedmen's Bureau and a number of religious groups moved into the state to handle the issue of the state's former slaves, but little was done toward assisting the rest of the population in pulling themselves back together, rebuilding families, and moving ahead. The first full year after the war saw intensified animosity toward former Unionists and the freedmen and those who were attempting to help them, including wartime Governor Isaac Murphy.²⁴⁹ The elections of 1866 saw voters put the old slate of pre-war candidates back in office.²⁵⁰ The federal congress looked

---

[248] Benjamin F. Webber and John Christian Wilson, Statements in support of the Homestead Application of The Heirs of James Baker, 25 August 1888, General Land Office, Bureau of Land Management, National Archives, Washington, DC.

[249] Murphy was the only holdout in the vote to secede during the second secession convention. He refused to change his vote even under extreme pressure to do so from the rest of the delegates prompting Mrs. Frederick Trapnall of Little Rock to throw a bouquet of roses from the balcony that landed at Murphy's feet. The gesture reportedly brought order to the crowd.

[250] DeBlack, *With Fire and Sword*, 148. The elections of 1866 occurred while the nation was attempting to consolidate the Union using the form of reconstruction proposed by President Lincoln and his successor President Johnson. In 1868 the federal government established Radical

considerably different, though, and with the election of a majority of Republicans determined to make the rebellious states pay for what they had done to the Union, Radical Reconstruction entered the picture.

In 1863, President Lincoln issued a Proclamation of Amnesty and Reconstruction, which allowed a group that constituted at least one-tenth the voting population in the 1860 election to form a new state government under the federal union. Murphy had led the movement to do just that and was steering the process along fairly well. Unfortunately, Lincoln's assassination ended any hope of his reconstruction measures ever being enacted. Radical Republicans, led by Thaddeus Stevens of Pennsylvania and Charles Sumner of Massachusetts, insisted on a more restrictive re-entry into the Union. One of the aspects most disquieting to the former Rebels was that they were restricted from voting while the newly freed former slaves were allowed the privilege. This resulted in the freedmen's votes being even more powerful in places such as Crittenden County where pre-war cotton plantations resulted in high numbers of African American voters. The results were that former Rebels felt more disenfranchised and their anger increased, especially among the poorer class of residents, those like Duncan Stalker, who were faring much worse than the former slaveholders in the state. Arkansans were not the only Southerners angered by Reconstruction. In the spring of 1866, a group of young men in Pulaski, Tennessee, formed a group they called the Ku Klux Klan. By April of '67, Klan groups were forming in Little Rock.[251] Within a few months the organization had found support in many communities across the state, including northeast Arkansas, with Crittenden County considered the

---

Reconstruction which prevented those who had served the Confederate government from voting or holding office.
[251] Ibid, 178.

most persistent.²⁵² It was to this situation that Duncan Stalker had returned from the war.

D. P. Upham was a former Union officer from Massachusetts who had served during the war in Arkansas. After the war ended he moved his family to Augusta in Woodruff County and succeeded in winning a seat in the state house representing Woodruff, St. Francis, and Crittenden counties. In order to deal with the upswing in Klan activity, the Arkansas General Assembly authorized the creation of a state militia which ended up being made up primarily of a few loyal Unionists and freedmen. Upham himself organized four companies in his congressional district, with one company each from Woodruff and St. Francis counties and two companies from Crittenden County.²⁵³ Upham announced his policy to drive the Klansmen from the area saying that for every Republican killed, he would kill ten of the other side. In a letter to his brother Henry dated August 28, 1868, Upham proclaimed, "we will whale hell out of the last one of them, and never allow one of them to return and live here. There is no other way ... nothing but good healthy square, honest killing would ever do them any good."²⁵⁴

Klan activity in the summer of 1868 was high. Reconstruction had taken the vote away from most of the former Confederates and the Fourteenth Amendment had given it to the freedmen. In an attempt to discourage Republican voting in the election, Klansmen had resorted to whippings, beatings, and murder with as many as two hundred individual episodes reported to the governor's office in the months leading up to the election. The election in November saw a record number of Republicans elected to the legislature, winning eighty-two of the eighty-three seats. Shortly afterward, Governor Clayton established martial law

---

²⁵² Ibid, 183.
²⁵³ Ibid, 197.
²⁵⁴ Charles J. Rector, "D.P. Upham, Woodruff County Carpetbagger," *The Arkansas Historical Quarterly*, (59:1, Spring 2000), 65.

in ten counties, and within a few days had extended it to four more, including Crittenden. After suppressing the Klan elements in Woodruff County, Upham and his militia moved first to Fulton County, where he reestablished civil authority and then on to Crittenden County where the local unit was being supported by Klansmen from across the river in Memphis.

On December 11, the Second Regiment of the Arkansas State Guard under the command of Col. James T. Watson, entered Crittenden County to put down the Klan.[255] According to a letter from Col. E.M. Main, who had helped to organize the two companies of Crittenden County Militia for the governor,

> ...the county was in a most deplorable state of disorder. In fact a reign of terror, intimidation, and murder prevailed. The vilest passions of the worst element of the community seemed to be aroused and bent on evil doing, and no one dared to raise voice or hand in protest.[256]

Local citizens were reported to be completely intimidated by the Klansmen. The militia rode in and took the Klansmen by surprise. They captured a number of them and moved into Marion to reestablish control of the town and the county. Armed Klan members from Memphis assisted the local unit in attempting to overrun the militia and had almost succeeded when six hundred members of Col. William Monks' Missouri Cavalry rode in and saved the day for the militia. By February of 1869 the Klan was defeated in Crittenden County, its

---

[255] Ibid, 71.

[256] Powell Clayton, *The Aftermath of the Civil War in Arkansas*. (New York City: The Neale Publishing Company, 1915), 135. According to Clayton, the Crittenden County Klansmen were led by former Crittenden Ranger commander, Colonel Josiah Francis Earle, who had led both Jasper and Duncan during their military careers. After the Klan was put down, Earle became successful in the timber business in the northwestern corner of the county in the area that is now the town of Earle.

members scattering into surrounding counties.[257] On March 21, 1869, martial law was finally lifted in Crittenden County, the last place it had been in effect. Order was restored throughout the state and the newly elected legislature moved to make the Ku Klux Klan illegal.

Historians report that the Klan virtually ceased to exist within the state during the rest of Reconstruction but a strong element of the group continued its activity without the official title in neighboring Mississippi County for several more years. In 1872, Klansmen led by former Confederate officer and Klan leader Captain Charles Bowen attacked a group of blacks who were supposedly part of one of the many secret fraternal organizations that were popular with both races. Local lore has it that a large group of black men had been participating in armed marches "making speeches and causing excitement" among the whites in the county. Bowen and his men attacked one such group, dispersing the crowd. While little information exists about the incident, known locally as the Black Hawk War, the attacks followed a shooting involving two county officials in which the county sheriff was killed. Over the next several days several blacks were killed in the Osceola area and many others left the county altogether.[258] With the end of Radical Reconstruction in 1874, the Democrats took control of the state government again, eventually ushering in Jim Crow in Arkansas. The Klan would lie dormant for the next forty years before they would resurface again in a much more visible manner.

---

[257] Ibid, 198. See also, William Monks, *A History of Southern Missouri and Northern Arkansas: Being an Account of the Early Settlements, the Civil War, the Ku-Klux, and Times of Peace.* (Fayetteville: University of Arkansas Press), 2003. Monks was a notorious guerilla on the Union side of the fight from Howell County, Missouri. In his book he states that when Gov. Clayton ordered him to disband his unit, which had been mustered into Arkansas state service to assist in putting down the uprising, he was presented with a new suit of clothes by the citizens of Marion.
[258] Mabel F. Edrington, *History of Mississippi County, Arkansas: 1962.* Ocala, Florida: Ocala Star-Banner, 1962, 366.

Ann Stalker's brother-in-law and at least one other neighbor place her in Poinsett County as early as 1867. Her oldest daughter told her children and grandchildren stories of traveling alone with her mother and brother to stake out a homestead, sleeping in a tent on the mound for the required number of days. It appears that she was a young widow with two small children when she came to the mound in the swamp in what is now Tyronza to attempt to homestead a farm near the home of her younger sister and brother-in-law.[259] From other family accounts related by Caroline, it also appears that she initially lived near her older sister Caroline and her husband John Roman on the Tyronza River near the Gibson Bayou community in Crittenden County. When her sister Caroline died, Ann apparently felt compelled to pull up stakes and move near her other sister, Paralee.

Poinsett County had a very small African American population at the time because the county was so sparsely populated and the area of greatest population, Crowley's Ridge, was not well suited to the type of farming that required large numbers of slaves. It was spared the type of civil breakdown that plagued counties such as Crittenden and Mississippi although Klansmen from surrounding counties visited the sheriff there. When the State Militia put down the Klan in the state, those who survived or remained at large fled

---

[259] Another record that I believe supports my theory is the 1900 Federal Census. That enumeration gathered information from women to determine fertility and child mortality rates. Ann stated that she had given birth to six children of which only two were surviving. Of the four known children she had in 1880, both Jimmy and Florence had died by 1900, leaving Caroline and Ella. Two other children are not accounted for in any census or in the family history written by Roger Haley Howard. Based on marriage and death dates for her first two husbands is it highly unlikely that these two children would have arrived during these marriages. Florence was born about 1870 and Ella in 1876. It was common for women of child bearing age to give birth about every two years and would account for the six year gap between these two children. If Duncan appeared after being run out of Crittenden County in 1869, then Caroline's memories are most definitely correct.

into the surrounding counties. It is at this time that I believe Duncan left Crittenden County and moved into neighboring Poinsett County to remain hidden from the militia. Many people that I have spoken with over the years have mentioned Klan activity and sympathy in the Tyronza area in its early years. Many of its earliest residents were former Confederate soldiers in opposition to the early businessmen in places like Marked Tree who generally hailed from the Midwest. In an 1895 issue of the Harrisburg *Modern News*, Tyronza is touted as being the most progressive and beautiful town in the county. I believe that Tyronza's early history may have been kept under wraps because of Duncan Stalker's involvement with the Klan after the war. This move seemed to establish a pattern of secrecy in the town that continued for decades.[260]

Although Ann was the widow of a Union soldier, the depredations that occurred during the later years of the war often turned sympathy from one side to the other. Paralee's marriage to Jasper may have sealed the deal for Ann. Tyronza's long history of secrecy, or at least aloofness, may not have begun after the Union was brought down in the town, but long before that organization was ever conceived. Tyronza very possibly may have been a Confederate community from the start which would explain why it has always been slightly apart from the other towns in the area. The mystery to the secrecy surrounding Tyronza's past may not lie as much in the Union as it did in the Klan.

I think that Duncan fled Crittenden County in late 1868 or early 1869 and located his former comrade-in-arms, Jasper Mullins. There he met Jasper's neighbor and widowed sister-in-law, Ann Pittman, and the two were soon married. I cannot locate a marriage license for the couple and it is possible that one simply does not exist. The area around Dead Timber

---

[260] Duncan Stalker may not have been the only Klansman in the area with Jasper Mullins and the hired man listed in Ann's household in the 1880 census, John Rushing also serving in the Conederate Army.

Church and cemetery in Mississippi County was known to be sympathetic to Klan activity although not drawing as much attention as its neighbor to the south until the Black Hawk War in 1872. Ann Stalker, her sister Paralee and maybe Jasper, as well as Ann's son-in-law, William Perkins are buried in the cemetery there. Duncan and Jimmy may also be buried there although I have long believed they were buried on the mound beside the railroad bed in Tyronza.[261] The couple could have been married by the minister there, himself possibly an ex-Confederate, or prehaps not even married officially at all. Such common law arrangements were not that unusual at the time, especially in remote areas where access to civil government was difficult as it would have been anyway in the swamps, and made more so with reconstruction. The reason for the couple not showing up in the 1870 census (which they should have because their oldest child was born that year) may not have been because they were accidentally missed in a sloppy enumeration, but because they were hiding. At the time, the government in Arkansas was still functioning under Radical Reconstruction, and Duncan would most likely have not wanted to be recognized by the government of the United States.

Radical Reconstruction came to an end in 1874 and business and politics as usual returned to Arkansas. Most of the progress made by blacks in the state during Reconstruction was erased, although many black landowners, businessmen, and professionals, continued to prosper through the Jim Crow period. Perhaps at this time, Duncan felt safe enough to reveal his location, as the first known records for the couple surface in April, 1876 when they officially purchased the land at

---

[261] Daughter Caroline may have chosen to bury her mother near her own first husband instead of on the mound in Tyronza. Dead Timber Cemetery, today known as Whitton Cemetery, seems to be the family cemetery for the Perkins family. Caroline herself was buried in the Tyronza Cemetery with her second husband Mark Howard.

Tyronza from N.B. Martis. According to Ella Stalker Thorp's family Bible, Duncan died in September of that same year. The 1880 census enumerator would find Ann and her family and a year later the railroad would find them as well. For the first time in many years Ann and her children would operate in what would pass as civilization.

Bibliography

Books and Articles:

Allen, Barbara and William Lynwood Montell. *From Memory to History: Using Oral Sources in Local Historical Research.* Nashville: The American Association for State and Local History, 1981.

Amato, Joseph A. *Rethinking Home: A Case for Writing Local History.* Berkeley: University of California Press, 2002.

American Red Cross. *The Ohio-Mississippi Valley Flood Disaster of 1937: Report of Relief Operations of the American Red Cross.* Washington, DC: American Red Cross, 1938.

Ayers, Edward L. *Southern Crossing: A History of the American South, 1877-1906.* New York: Oxford University Press, 1998.

Bailey, Garrick. "Continuity and Change in Mississippian Civilization," in *Hero, Hawk, and Open Hand: American Indian Art of the Ancient Midwest and South.* ed. Richard . Townsend. New Haven: Yale University Press, 2004, pp. 83-91.

Barry, John M. *Rising Tide: The Great Mississippi River Flood of 1927 and How It Changed America.* New York: Touchstone Books, 1997.

Barry, John M. *The Great Influenza: The Epic Story of the Deadliest Plague in History.*, New York: Penguin Books, 2005.

Berry, Wendell. *The Unsettling of America: Culture and Agriculture.* San Francisco: Sierra Club Books, 1977.

Biegart, M. Langley. "Legacy of Resistance: Uncovering the History of Collective Action by Black Agricultural Workers in Central East Arkansas from the 1860's to the

1930's," in *Journal of Social History.* 32:1 (Autumn 1998), pp. 73-99.

Bolsterli. Margaret Jones. *Vinegar Pie and Chicken Bread: A Woman's Diary of Life in the Rural South, 1890-1891.* Fayetteville, University of Arkansas Press, 1982.

Bolsterli, Margaret Jones. *Born in the Delta: Reflections on the Making of a Southern White Sensibility.* Fayetteville: University of Arkansas, 2000.

Bolsterli, Margaret Jones. *During Wind and Rain: The Jones Family Farm in the Arkansas Delta, 1848-2006.* Fayetteville: University of Arkansas Press, 2008.

Bradbury, John F. and Lou Wehmer. "William Monks: Union Guerilla and Memoirist," in *A History of Southern Missouri and Northern Arkansas: Being an Account of the Early Settlements, the Civil War, the Ku-Klux, and Times of Peace.* Fayetteville: University of Arkansas Press, 2003, pp. ix-lxvii.

Brown, Ian. "Cyrus Thomas and the Mound Explorations of the Bureau of Ethnology," in *Edward Palmer's Arkansaw Mounds,* ed. Marvin W. Jeter, Fayetteville: University of Arkansas Press, 1990, pp. 23-27.

Bunkse, Edmunds Valdemars. *Geography and the Art of Life.* Baltimore: The Johns Hopkins University Press, 2004.

Carr, Patrick J. and Maria J. Kefalas. *Hollowing Out the Middle: The Rural Brain Drain and What It Means for America.* Boston: Beacon Press, 2009.

Carson, James Taylor. *Searching for the Bright Path: The Mississippi Choctaws from Prehistory to Removal.* Lincoln: University of Nebraska Press, 1999.

Carson, Rachel. *Silent Spring.* Boston: Houghton-Mifflin, 2002.

Clayton, Lawrence A., Vernon James Knight, Jr., and Edward C Moore, eds. *The De Soto Chronicles: The Expedition of Hernando de Soto to North America in 1539-1543, Volume 1.* Tuscaloosa: University of Alabama Press, 1993.

Clayton, Powell. *The Aftermath of the Civil War in Arkansas.* New York City: The Neale Publishing Company, 1915.

Cobb, James C. *The Most Southern Place on Earth: The Mississippi Delta and the Roots of Regional Identity.* New York: Oxford University Press, 1992.

Cobb, James C. *The South and America since World War II.* New York: Oxford University Press, 2011.

Coffman, Jerry L., Carl A. von Hake, and Carl W. Stover. *Earthquake History of the United States.* Boulder: United States Department of Commerce, 1982.

Collier, Major Calvin L., USAF (Ret.). *The War Child's Children: A Story of the Third Arkansas Cavalry.* Little Rock: Pioneer Press, 1965.

Crawford, Alan Pell. *Twilight at Monticello: The Final Years of Thomas Jefferson.* New York: Random House, 2008.

Cronon, William, ed. *Uncommon Ground: Rethinking the Human Place in Nature.* New York: W.W. Norton & Co., 1995.

Danbom, David B. *Born in the Country: A History of Rural America.* Baltimore: Johns Hopkins University Press, 1995.

Daniel, Pete. *Lost Revolutions: The South in the 1950's.* Chapel Hill: University of North Carolina Press, 2000.

Daniel. Pete. *Toxic Drift: Pesticides and Health in the Post-World War II South.* Baton Rouge: Louisiana State University Press, 2005.

Daniel, Pete. "The Transformation of the Rural South; 1930 to the Present," in *Agricultural History,* 55: 3 (July, 1981), pp. 231-248.

Daniel, Pete. "Going Among Strangers: Southern Reactions to World War II," in *The Journal of American History,* 71: 3 (Dec, 1990) pp. 886-911.

Daniels, Jonathan. *A Southerner Discovers the South.* New York: DeCapo Press, 1970.

Davenport, Guy. *The Geography of the Imagination.* San Francisco: North Point Press, 1984.

Davidson, Osha Gray. *Broken Heartland: The Rise of America's Rural Ghetto.* Iowa City: University of Iowa Press, 1996.

Davies, Pete. *American Road: The Story of an Epic Transcontinental Journey at the Dawn of the Motor Age.* New York: Henry Holt and Company, 2002.

Davies, Richard. "Introduction" in *Rethinking Home: A Case for Writing Local History,* by Joseph A. Amato. Berkeley: University of California Press, 2002, pp. xiii-xvi.

Dawson, David D. "Baseball Calls: Arkansas Town Baseball in the Twenties", in *The Arkansas Historical Quarterly,* 43:4 (Winter, 1995), pp. 409-26.

Dean, Virgil W. *An Opportunity Lost: The Truman Administration and the Farm Policy Debate.* Columbia: University of Missouri Press, 2006.

DeBlack, Thomas A. *With Fire and Sword: Arkansas, 1861-1874.* Fayetteville: University of Arkansas Press, 2003.

Demuth, David O. "The Burning of Hopefield," in *The Arkansas Historical Quarterly,* 36:3 (Summer, 1977), pp. 123-129.

Derreault, Melanie. "American Wilderness and First Contact," in *American Wilderness: A New History.* Michael Lewis, ed. New York: Oxford University Press, 2007.

Dougan, Michael B. *Confederate Arkansas: The People and Politics of a Frontier State in Wartime* Tuscaloosa: University of Alabama Press, 1976.

Dunbar, Anthony. *Against the Grain: Southern Radicals and Prophets, 1929-1959.* Charlottesville: University of Virginia Press, 1981.

East, Charles. "The Delta" in *Place in American Fiction: Excursions and Explorations.* eds. H.L. Weatherby and George Core. Columbia: University of Missouri Press, 2004, pp. 46-59.

Edgerton, John. *Speak Now Against the Day: The Generation Before the Civil Rights Movement in the South.* Chapel Hill: University of North Carolina Press, 1995.

Edrington, Mabel F. *History of Mississippi County, Arkansas: 1962.* Ocala, Florida: Ocala Star-Banner, 1962.

Ellenberg, George B. *Mule South to Tractor South: Mules, Machines, and the Transformation of the Cotton South.* Tuscaloosa: University of Alabama Press, 2007.

Emerson, Robert M., Rachel I. Fretz, and Linda L. Shaw. *Writing Ethnographic Fieldnotes.* Chicago: University of Chicago Press, 1995.

Fagan, Brian. *The Little Ice Age: How Climate Made History, 1300-1850.* New York: Basic Books, 2000.

Falk, William W., Clarence B. Talley, and Bruce R. Rankin. "Life in the Forgotten South: The Black Belt," in *Forgotten Places: Uneven Development in Rural America.* Thomas A. Lyson and William W. Falk, eds. Lawrence: University Press of Kansas, 1993, pp. 53-75.

Faragher, John Mack. *Sugar Creek: Life on the Illinois Prairie.* New haven: Yale University Press, 1986.

Fitchen, Janet M. *Endangered Spaces, Enduring Places: Change, Identity, and Survival in Rural America.* Boulder: Westview Press, 1991.

Foucault, Michel. *Discipline and* Punish. New York: Vintage Books, 1995.

Freshwater, David. *Rural America at the Turn of the Century.* University of Kentucky TVA Rural Studies Program, 1999.

Gaddis, John Lewis. *The Landscape of History: How Historians Map the Past.* New York: Oxford University Press, 2002.

Gatewood, Willard B. "The Arkansas Delta: Deepest of the Deep South," in *The Arkansas Delta: Land of Paradox.* Jeannie M Whayne and Carl H. Moneyhon, eds. Fayetteville: University of Arkansas Press, 1993, pp. 3-29.

Gay, James Thomas. "Norman Thomas: Tribune of the Disenfranchased," in *The Arkansas Historical Quarterly.* 48:4 (Winter 1989), pp. 329-348.

Gordon, John Steele. *An Empire of Wealth: The Epic History of American Economic Power.* New York: Harper Perennial, 2004.

Gray, James L. and Dick V. Ferguson. *Soil Survey of Poinsett County, Arkansas.* Washington, DC: United States Department of Agriculture, 1977.

Gray, John. *Arkansas Forest History.*[online] Little Rock: Arkansas Forestry Association, 1995. Accessed January 8, 2011); available from <http://arkforests.org/resources-foresthistory/html>; Internet.Greene, Alison Collis. 2010. No depression in heaven: Religion and economic crisis in Memphis and the delta, 1929-1941.Yale University. In PROQUESTMS ProQuest Dissertations & Theses (PQDT), http://search.proquest.com/docview/847395750?accountid=8363.

Hamilton, Mary. *Trials of the Earth: the Autobiography of Mary Hamilton.* Helen Dick Davis, ed. Jackson: University Press of Mississippi, 1992.

Hanson, Gerald T. and Carl Moneyhon. *Historical Atlas of Arkansas.* Norman: University of Oklahoma Press, 1981.

Heard, Kenneth. "Tyronza working to secure wall for Vietnam veterans", in *Arkansas Democrat-Gazette,* December 25, 2011, p. 1B.

Heppen, John and Samuel M. Otterstrom, eds. *Geography, History, and the American Political Economy.* Lanham: Lexington Books, 2009.

Hobson, Fred, ed.. *South to the Future: An American Region in the Twenty-First Century.* Athens: University of Georgia Press, 2002.

Holley, Donald. *Uncle Sam's Farmers: The New Deal Communities in the Lower Mississippi Valley.* Urbana: University of Illinois Press, 1975.

Hooks, Bell. *Belonging: A culture of place.* New York: Routledge, 2009.

Hong, Keumsoo. "The Structural Transformation of the Antebellum Red River Valley Settlement Systems in Louisiana." In *Geography, History, and the American*

Political Economy. ed. John Heppen and Samuel M. Otterstrom. Lanham: Lexington Books, 2009., pp. 65-97.

Howard, Roger Haley. *Descendants of David Anthony Pittman: Seven Generations.* Little Rock: self-published, 1984.

Howe, Tony. "Arkansas Logging Railroads." Logging Railroads of North America. <http://www.loggingrailroads.com/ar.htm> (accessed February 23, 2012).

Hudson, Charles. *Knights of Spain, Warriors of the Sun: Hernando de Soto and the South's Ancient Chiefdoms.* Athens: The University of Georgia Press, 1997.

Huff, Leo E. "Jayhawkers and Bushwackers in Northern Arkansas During the Civil War," in *The Arkansas Historical Quarterly.* 24:2 (Summer 1965), pp. 127-148.

Hyland, Stanley and Michael Timberlake. "The Mississippi Delta: Change or Continued Trouble," in *Forgotten Places: Uneven Development in Rural America.* Thomas A. Lyson and William W. Falk, eds. Lawrence: University Press of Kansas, 1993, pp. 76-101.

Jackson, Bruce. *Fieldwork.* Urbana: University of Illinois Press, 1987.

Jakle, John A. *The American Small Town: Twentieth Century Place Images.* Hamden, CT: Archon Books, 1982.

Jaquish, Barbara. 2008. "An examination of the mythic frameworks used by two forms of media to present the southern tenant farmers union." University of Arkansas. In PROQUESTMS ProQuest Dissertations & Theses (PQDT), http://search.proquest.com/docview/304686907?accountid=8363.

Jennings, Francis. *The Invasion of America: Indians, Colonialism, and the Cant of Conquest.* Chapel Hill: University of North Carolina Press, 2010.

Jeter, Marvin D., ed. *Edward Palmer's Arkansaw Mounds.* Fayetteville: University of Arkansas Press, 1990.

Jeter, Marvin D. and Dan F. Morse. "Nearly Destroyed: Palmer's Last Work in Northeast Arkansas, Late 1883," in *Edward Palmer's Arkansaw Mounds,* ed. Marvin W. Jeter, Fayetteville: University of Arkansas Press, 1990, pp. 344-51.

Kiser, G. Gregory. "The Socialist Party in Arkansas, 1900-1912", in *The Arkansas Historical Quarterly,*40:2 (Summer, 1981), pp. 119-153.

Lemann, Nicholas. *The Promised Land: The Great Black Migration and How It Changed America.* New York: A.A. Knopf, 1991.

LeMaster, Carolyn Gray. *A Corner of the Tapestry: A History of the Jewish Experience in Arkansas, 1820-1990.* Fayetteville: University of Arkansas Press, 1994.

Lewis, Michael. *American Wilderness: A New History.* New York: Oxford University Press, 2007.

Linklater, Andro. *The Fabric of America: How Our Borders and Boundaries Shaped the Country and Forged Our National Identity.* New York: Walker and Company, 2007.

Lingeman, Richard. *Small Town America: A Narrative History.* New York: G.P. Putnam's Sons, 1980.

Longnecker, Julia Ward. "A Road Divided: From Memphis to Little Rock Through the Great Mississippi Swamp," in *The Arkansas Historical Quarterly,* 44:3, (Autumn 1985) pp. 203-219.

Lyson, Thomas A. and William W. Falk. "Poor Rural Regions in the United States," in *Forgotten Places: Uneven Development in Rural America.* Thomas A. Lyson and William W. Falk, eds. Lawrence: University Press of Kansas, 1993, pp. 1-6.

Mackey, Robert R. (Maj.). *The Uncivil War: Irregular Warfare in the Upper South, 1861-1865.* Norman: University of Oklahoma Press, 2004.

Manthorne, Jason. "The View from the Cotton: Reconsidering the Southern Tenant Farmers Union," in *Agricultural History* 84:1, Jan 2010, pp. 20-45.

Martin, Robert F. *Howard Kester and the Struggle for Social Justice in the South, 1904-77.* Charlottesville: The University Press of Virginia Press, 1991.

Million, Michael G. "A Preliminary Field Study of the Archeological Resources of a Four Mile Portion of the Tyronza River, Poinsett County, Arkansas," in *Contract Archeology in the Lower Mississippi Valley of Arkansas: Miscellaneous Papers.* Timothy C. Klinger, ed. Fayetteville: Arkansas Archeological Survey, 1977, pp. 84-104.

Mitchell, H. L. *Roll the Union On: A Pictorial History of the Southern Tenant Farmers' Union.* Chicago: Charles H. Kerr Publishing Company, 1987.

Mitchell, H.L. *Mean Things Happening in this Land: The Life and Times of H.L. Mitchell, Co-Founder of the Southern Tenant Farmers Union.* Norman: University of Oklahoma Press, 2008.

Moneyhon, Carl H. *Arkansas and the New South, 1874-1929.* Fayetteville: University of Arkansas Press, 1997.

Moneyhon, Carl H. "Delta Towns: Their Rise and Decline," in *The Arkansas Delta: Land of Paradox.* Jeannie M Whayne and Carl H. Moneyhon, eds. Fayetteville: University of Arkansas Press, 1993, pp. 208-237.

Monks, William. *A History of Southern Missouri and Northern Arkansas: Being an Account of the Early Settlements, the Civil War, the Ku-Klux, and Times of Peace.* Fayetteville: University of Arkansas Press, 2003.

Morse, Phyllis A. *Parkin: The 1978-1979 Archeological Investigations of a Cross County, Arkansas Site.* Fayetteville: Arkansas Archeological Survey, 1981.

Mosher, Anne E. "Earle's Theory and Conception of the Geographical History of the United States," in *Geography, History, and the American Political Economy.* ed. John

Heppen and Samuel M. Otterstrom. Lanham: Lexington Books, 2009., pp. 7-17.

O'Brien, Michael J. and Robert C. Dunnell, eds. *Changing Perspectives on the Archaeology of the Central Mississippi River Valley.* Tuscaloosa: University of Alabama Press, 1998.

O'Connor, Carol A. *A Sort of Utopia: Scarsdale, 1891-1981.* Albany: State University of New York Press, 1983.

O'Daniel, Patrick. *Memphis and the Super flood of 1937: High Water Blues.* Charleston: The History Press, 2010.

Oldenburg, Ray. *The Great Good Place: Cafes, Coffee Shops, Bookstores, Bars, Hair Salons, and Other Hangouts at the Heart of a Community.* Cambridge: DaCapo Press, 1997.

Otto, John Solomon. *The Final Frontier,1880-1930: Settling the Southern Bottomlands.* Westport: Greenwood Press, 1999.

Payne, Elizabeth Anne. "The Lady was a Sharecropper," in *Southern Cultures*, 4:2 (Summer 1998), pp. 5-28.

Pritchett, Merrill R. and William L. Shea. "The Afrika Korps in Arkansas, 1943-1946," in *The Arkansas Histroical Quarterly*, 37:1 (Spring, 1978), pp. 3-22.

Rector, Charles J. "D.P. Upham, Woodruff County Carpetbagger, in *The Arkansas Historical Quarterly*, 59:1 (Spring, 2000), pp. 59-75.

Reed, John Shelton. *Minding the South.* Columbia: University of Missouri Press, 2003.

Ritter, Anna. "Marked Tree from 1883-1936" in *Marked Tree Tribune*, July 17, 1939, p. 24-7.

Roberts, Bobby and Carl Moneyhon. *Portraits of Conflict: A Photographic History of Arkansas in the Civil War.* Fayetteville: University of Arkansas Press, 1987.

Roll, Jared. *Spirit of Rebellion: Labor and Religion in the New Cotton South.* Urbana: University of Illinois Press, 2010.

Ross, James D., Jr. "'I ain't got no home in this world': The Rise and Fall of the Southern Tenant Farmers' Union in Arkansas." PhD diss., Auburn University, 2004.

Ross, Margaret. "The New Madrid Earthquake," in *The Arkansas Historical Quarterly*. 27:2 (Summer, 1968) pp. 83-104.

Rushing, Wanda. *Memphis and the Paradox of Place: Globalization in the American South*. Chapel Hill: University of North Carolina Press, 2009.

Saikku, Mikko. This Delta, This Land: An Environmental History of the Yazoo-Mississippi Floodplain. Athens: University of Georgia Press, 2005.

Schama, Simon. *Landscape and Memory*. New York: Alred A. Knopf, 1995.

Shea, William L. "A Semi-Savage State: The Image of Arkansas in the Civil War," in *Civil War Arkansas: Beyond Battles and Leaders*. Anne J. Bailey and Daniel E. Sutherland, eds. Fayetteville: University of Arkansas Press, 2000, pp. 85-99.

Shepard, Edward M. "The New Madrid Earthquake," in *The Journal of Geology* 13:1 (Jan-Feb 1905) pp. 45-62.

Sherman, Jennifer. *Those Who Work, Those Who don't: Poverty, Morality, and Family in Rural America*. Minneapolis: University of Minnesota Press, 2009.

Smith, Bruce D. "Agricultural Chiefdoms of the Eastern Woodlands" in *The Cambridge History of the Native Peoples of the Americas, Volume I: North America*, Bruce G. Trigger and Wilcomb E. Washburn, eds. New York: Cambridge University Press, 1996, pp. 267-324.

Smith, Bruce D. "The Division of Mound Exploration of the Bureau of Ethnology and the Birth of Modern American Archeology," in in *Edward Palmer's Arkansaw Mounds*, ed. Marvin W. Jeter, Fayetteville: University of Arkansas Press, 1990, pp. 27-37.

Smith, C. Calvin. *War and Wartime Changes: The Transformation of Arkansas, 1940-1945*. Fayetteville: University of Arkansas Press, 1986.

Smith, Kimberly. *Wendell Berry and the Agrarian Tradition: A Common Grace.* Lawrence: University Press of Kansas, 2003.

Steinberg, Ted. *Down to Earth: Nature's Role in American History.* Oxford: Oxford University Press, 2002.

Straw, Richard A. *High Mountains Rising: Appalachia in Time and Place.* Urbana: University of Illinois Press, 2004.

Sutherland, Daniel E. "Guerillas: The Real War in Arkansas," in *Civil War Arkansas: Beyond Battles and Leaders.* Anne J. Bailey and Daniel E. Sutherland, eds. Fayetteville: University of Arkansas Press, 2000, pp. 133-153.

Sutter, Ruth E. *The Next Place You Come To: A Historical Introduction to North America.* Englewood Cliffs, NJ: Prentice-Hall, Inc., 1973.

Swank, Roy. *Trail to Marked Tree.* San Antonio: Naylor Company, 1968.

Theobald, Paul. *Teaching the Commons: Place, Pride, and the Renewal of Community.* Boulder: Westview Press, 1997.

Thomas, Cyrus. *Report on the Mound Explorations of the Bureau of Ethnology.* Washington, DC: Smithsonian Institution Press, 1985.

Toney, James T. "A Preliminary Field Study of the Archeological and Historical Resources of an Eight Mile Portion of the Tyronza River," in *Contract Archeology in the Lower Mississippi Valley of Arkansas: Miscellaneous Papers.* Timothy C. Klinger, ed. Fayetteville: Arkansas Archeological Survey, 1977, pp. 105-131.

Townsend, Richard F. "American Landscapes, Seen and Unseen," in *Hero, Hawk, and Open Hand: American Indian Art of the Ancient Midwest and South.* ed. Richard . Townsend. New Haven: Yale University Press, 2004, pp. 15-35.

Van Arsdale, Roy and Randel T. Cox. "The Mississippi's Curious Origins," in *Scientific American*, 296:1 (January 2007) 76-82B. *Academic Search Complete*, EBSCOhost (accessed September 8, 2010).

Ventkateramani, M.S. "Norman Thomas, Arkansas Sharecroppers, and the Roosevelt Agricultural Policies, 1933-1937," in *The Arkansas Historical Quarterly*, 24:1, (Spring 1965), pp. 3-28.

Von Hesse-Wartegg, Ernst. *Travels on the Lower Mississippi, 1879-1880: A Memoir by Ernst von Hesse-Wartegg*. Frederic Trautmann, ed. Columbia: University of Missouri Press, 1990.

Wallace, Henry A. *Corn and Corn Growing*. New York: John Wiley and Sons, Inc., 1937.

Wallach, Bret. *Understanding the Cultural Landscape*. New York: Guilford Press, 2005.

Walter, Eugene Victor. *Placeways: A Theory of the Human Environment*. Chapel Hill: University of North Carolina Press, 1988.

Ward, Jason Morgan. "Nazis Hoe Cotton: Planters, POW's, and the Future of Farm Labor in the Deep South," in *Agricultural History*, 81:4 (Fall, 2007), 471-492.

Welty, Eudora. *One Time, One Place: Mississippi in the Depression, a Snapshot Album*. Jackson: University of Mississippi Press, 1996.

Welty, Eudora. *Some Notes on River Country*. Jackson: University of Mississippi Press, 2003.

Whayne, Jeannie M. *A New Plantation South: Land, Labor, and Federal Favor in Twentieth Century Arkansas*. Charlottesville: University Press of Virginia, 1996.

Whayne, Jeannie M. "Creation of a Plantation System in the Arkansas," Delta in the Twentieth Century," in *Agricultural History*, 66:1 (Winter, 1992), 63-84.

Whayne, Jeannie M. and Willard B. Gatewood. *The Arkansas Delta: Land of Paradox*. Fayetteville: University of Arkansas Press, 1993.

Whayne, Jeannie M. "Robert E. Lee Wilson and the Making of a Post-Civil War Plantation," in *the Southern Elite and Social Change: Essays in Honor of Willard B. Gatewood, Jr.*, Randy Finley and Thomas A. DeBlack, eds.

Fayetteville: University of Arkansas Press, 2002, pp. 95-117.

Whitaker, Robert. *On the Laps of Gods: The Red Summer of 1919 and the Struggle for Justice that Remade a Nation.* New York: Crown Publishers, 2008.

Williamson, Joel. "Southern Genius in the Twentieth Century," in *South* to the Future: An American Region in the Twenty-First Century, ed. Fred Hobson. Athens: University of Georgia Press, 2002, pp. 13-24.

Winne, Mark. *Closing the Food Gap: Resetting the Table in the Land of Plenty.* Boston: Beacon Press, 2008.

Wood, Richard E. *Survival of Rural America: Small Victories and Bitter Harvests.* Lawrence: University Press of Kansas, 2008.

Woodruff, Nan Elizabeth. "Pick or Fight: The Emergency Farm Labor Program in the Arkansas and Mississippi Deltas During World War II," in *Agricultural History,* 64: 2, The United States Department of Agriculture in Historical Perspective (Spring, 1990), pp. 74-85.

Woods, Jeff. *Red Scare, Black Struggle: Segregation and Anti-Communism in the South, 1948-1968.*Baton Rouge: Louisiana State University Press, 2004.

Wulf, Andrea. *Founding Gardeners: The Revolutionary Generation, Nature, and the Shaping of the American Nation.* New York: Alfred A. Knopf, 2011.

Youngblood, Joshua C. "Realistic Religion and Radical Prophets: The STFU, the Social Gospel, and the American Left in the 1930's," Master's thesis, Florida State University, 2004.

Newspapers:

Arkansas Democrat
Arkansas Gazette
Atlanta Daily World

Capitol Plaindealer (Topeka, KS)
Chicago Defender
Commonwealth College Fortnightly
Danville (VA) Bee
Kingsport (TN) Times
Marked Tree Tribune
Memphis Commercial-Appeal
Negro Star (Wichita, KS)
New York Times
Northwest Arkansas Times
Osceola (AR) Times
Parkin (AR) Free Press
Parkin (AR) Times
Plaindealer (Kansas City, KS)
Syracuse (N.Y.) Herald
The Wall Street Journal
Wyandotte Echo (Kansas City, KS)

Archival Collections:

Henry Clay East Papers. University of Arkansas Special Collections
Southern Tenant Farmers Union Papers, 1934-1977. ProQuest
Southern Tenant Farmers Union Photographs, 1937 and 1982. Kheel Center Labor Photos, Cornell University.
The Green Rising: Supplement to the Southern Tenant Farmers Union Papers, 1910-1977. ProQuest
Tyronza Ginning Company Papers: (John Adam Emrich and John H. Emrich). University of Arkansas Special Collections.

Government Documents:

Homestead Application for The Heirs of James Baker, General Land Office, Bureau of Land Management, National Archives, Washington, DC.

Homestead Application for The Heirs of Thomas J. Hudson, General Land Office, Bureau of Land Management, National Archives, Washington, DC.

Tenth Census of the United States, (1880) Little River Township, Poinsett County, Arkansas.

Twelfth Census of the United States, (1900) Tyronza Township, Poinsett County, Arkansas.

Thirteenth Census of the United States, (1910) Tyronza Township, Poinsett County, Arkansas.

Fourteenth Census of the United States, (1920) Tyronza Township, Poinsett County, Arkansas.

Fifteenth Census of the United States, (1930) Tyronza City and Township, Poinsett County, Arkansas.

Oral History:

John Russell Butler, Southern Historical Collection, University of North Carolina.
Minnie Damron, Southern Tenant Farmers Museum Collection.
Henry Clay East, Southern Historical Collection, University of North Carolina.
Jack East, Southern Tenant Farmers Museum Collection.
Dr. Eldon Fairley, Southern Tenant Farmers Museum Collection.
Robert Andrew Jackson, Southern Tenant Farmers Museum Collection.
John St. John, Southern Tenant Farmers Museum Collection.
Harry Leland (H.L.) Mitchell, Southern Tenant Farmers Union Collection, University of Texas-Arlington.
Samuel Howard Mitchell, Southern Tenant Farmers Museum Collection.
Orin Delaney Pendergast, Southern Tenant Farmers Museum Collection.
Johnny Rye, Southern Tenant Farmers Museum Collection.

John Twist, Southern Tenant Farmers Museum Collection.
Alma East Willoughby, Southern Tenant Farmers Museum Collection.

Personal Interviews and Conversations:

These conversations were not formal interviews, but simply conversations that took place over time. Extensive field notes were kept, although not recorded during the conversation, but later as a way of collecting my thoughts.

John Wayne Austin, Tyronza, Arkansas
George Beley, Tyronza, Arkansas
Judy Perry Black, Cherry Valley, Arkansas
Marion Burks, Tyronza, Arkansas
Linda Pitts Hinton, Tyronza, Arkansas
Edwin Perry, Cherry Valley, Arkansas
W.R. "Teddy" Prestige, Tyronza, Arkansas
Barbara Ross, Tyronza, Arkansas
Thelma Jones Jett, Tyronza, Arkansas
Calvin McDaniel, Houston, Texas
Lucy McDaniel Woodruff, Aiken, South Carolina
Louise (Soozi) Williams, Marked Tree, Arkansas
Mary Ann Ritter Arnold, Marked Tree, Arkansas

Made in the USA
Charleston, SC
06 February 2014